VISIONS of
GLORY

VISIONS of GLORY

Studies in the
Book of
Revelation

David J. Wieand

The Brethren Press, Elgin, Ill.

Library of Congress Cataloging in Publication Data
Wieand, David J., 1914-
    Visions of Glory
      1. Bible. New Testament. Revelation—Commentaries.
I. Title.
BS2825.3.W52   228′.07   79-9294
ISBN 0-87178-905-1

Contents

Preface

This book is intended for use by youth and adult groups. It is written out of the strong conviction that the way to understand Revelation is to let the book speak for itself. Do not use commentaries or other books on Revelation. This is the basic way to avoid controversy and find the message of Revelation for today.

The place for the use of commentaries is much later—after you have studied the entire book and understood its message. To help you in this process, the present writer with few exceptions has avoided references to other books and even to other books of the Bible. For the same reason he has avoided entering into debates about the meaning of details of the visions. The details of the visions are the brush strokes of the artist and are important only as they contribute to the central message of the vision.

John understood his book to be a witness to the Word of God (1:2). It still needs to be asked, How should Revelation be interpreted? Should it be interpreted: (1) as literal history; (2) as a letter to seven actual Christian congregations in the latter part of the first century; (3) as an outline of church history from John's day to ours; (4) as symbolism not to be taken literally but as containing spiritual truth; (5) as being dictated by God, Christ, or the Holy Spirit?

Whatever answer is given to these questions, it is nevertheless imperative that Revelation should be interpreted as great religious art. Great art touches the deep chords of eternal truth. It possesses a universal quality that transcends the specific time, place, and conditions of its origin. There is an unconditioned aspect to it that has the power to speak to any person who will give it ear. It carries the unmistakable ring of truth. Thus it is valid for all times and all seasons and all manner of men and women.

Our privilege is to listen with out total being. It is not enough to listen with the ears, for we shall miss what the eye and heart can tell us—nor with the mind alone, for in our preoccupation with reason and logic, we shall miss the overtones of the deep steady heartbeat of the Spirit. To truly listen we must use that unique gift of the human spirit, the imagination. For God has granted the imagination and the power to recreate, yes, to bring to life in our own life, being, and experience the truth that the artist implanted in his chosen medium.

Our re-creation can never match the original masterpiece point for point. Nor can a son, however much he adores his father, become an exact copy of his dad. A wooden, lifeless imitation is not what is needed. What is needed is a living, vibrant re-creation in which the very being of the interpreter meets the creative spirit of the artist embodied in his work. To use another figure, when Sir George Solti conducts a Chicago Symphony rendition of Beethoven's *Ninth Symphony* it must first of all be genuine Beethoven. But *it must also be Maestro Solti!* The concert program, however faithful or abortive the production has been, always carries the name of the conductor.

A genuine work of art has more to say than it can explicitly embody. There is that archetypal element in it of which the artist is only dimly aware. The artist who, when asked about the meaning of his work, sincerely says, "What does it say to you?" is probing the depths of his own soul.

And so we come to the Book of Revelation. What is the functional impact of Revelation? Revelation moves people more by an appeal to the heart than to the mind. The language of liturgy is at home here. Hymns, visual imagery, incense, metaphor, mystery, symbols are the materials with which John the artist works. The canvas on which John paints is vast. The colors are brilliant. The tremendous sounds resound to the four corners of the universe. The stupendous, decisive action John portrays strains the capacity of the imaginations of his hearers to their utmost limits.

Revelation fits the occasion for which it was written: the worship service on the Lord's day in the churches of Asia Minor. As the reader reads aloud the prophecy from John, the hearer in his imagination sees the Glorified Christ standing in the midst of the candelabra of his own congregation. He hears Christ speaking to his people who stand there expectantly awaiting the divine message. He is moved to worship and praise. "Worthy is the Lamb that was slain, to receive power and wealth and wisdom and might and honor and glory and blessing!" shouts the reader. And the assembled congregation bows down and replies, "Amen!"

John's story is at once the presentation of the faith of the congregation and the anticipatory fulfillment of its eschatological hope. The repetitive adoration of God's omnipotence, of his creative and sustaining power, of his holiness, his worth, and his kingship builds up a cumulative affirmation and welling up of the heart. And God's presence is experienced within the worshiping community. The rehearsal over and over of the redemptive death of the Lamb which "made us a kingdom of priests to God" reinforces in the hearts of the worshiping faithful the certainty of their own salvation. John's repeated colorful painting of the existential struggle with Satan and the "kings of the earth" experienced in miniature by the worshipers enables the imagination to experience the "not yet" as present. Through John's evocative pictures repeated again and again in different colors and re-occurring motifs, the final victory of God the Almighty and of the Lamb slain before the foundation of the world is experienced as certain and felt to be present. The expectant believers, caught up in the exaltation of the moment, become a part of that great company of the faithful martyrs who surround the throne of God and chant praises to the Almighty. They are moved to repentance and are ready to be "faithful unto death." For in their hearts they know that Christ reigns and that they shall receive the crown of life.

And so it is with us today. As we read John's Revelation, listen to his angelic choruses, see the vast canvas on which he works, our memory banks of faith are tapped, the crucified and resurrected Christ of the Gospels, of Paul, of the theologians, of our own religious story becomes real. Our hearts burn within us in faith, in adoration, and in praise.

It is but a small step for the religious imagination flamed by John's visions to leap from the present into the future. From the victory won by Christ on the cross to his final victory over Satan, we move through identifying with him to our final victory over the limitations of this life to the glories of the life beyond death.

Is Revelation a message sent and intended for seven historical churches in Asia Minor in the first century? Yes, for we must be faithful to the text. Is Revelation only a message sent and intended for seven historical churches in Asia Minor in the first century? No, for Revelation embodies eternal truths about God's saving purpose for men and women of every age — God's saving purpose accomplished and confirmed by the life, death, and resurrection of Jesus Christ.

The task of every interpreter of Revelation is so to enter into the life and thought of the prophet John that the eternal truths come to life again in the faith, the life, and proclamation of the interpreter.

Implications for Teacher and Student

The foregoing thesis has important implications for teacher and student. It is imperative that the teachers first of all open their hearts, imaginations, and minds to the great visions of Revelation if their students are going to be moved by its truth. If they are to understand the tremendous message of Revelation they must imaginatively enter into its content. They must see the door open into heaven. They must ascend with John and see the magnificence of him who is seated on the throne. They must in awe and reverence join the four living creatures, the four and twenty elders, the myriads of angels, and "every creature in heaven, and on earth and under the earth" and sing, "Worthy is the Lamb who was slain to receive power and wealth and wisdom and might and honor and glory and blessing!" Imaginative participation in the vision will bring the power of the Word of God in Revelation into the life of the participant. God's Word will claim loyalty, require commitment and inspire faith.

How to Teach Revelation

1. It is important for both teacher and student to study carefully the introductory chapter, "The Problem and the Glory of the Book of Revelation." You will want to go over carefully the points that are made. Place these on newsprint. Keep the newsprint posted for at least the first three sessions.

2. It is even more important to enable the class to visualize the visions of Revelation. They will need help at this point. As children they had active, healthy imaginations. You can help them rediscover their imaginations by actively involving them in the process.

First, get the facts. Who is involved? Where does the vision take place? What happens? First? Second? Third? Use repetition. John does. It takes time to see the vision. When the facts are clear, ask the class to close their eyes and see the vision in their imagination as you retell it. On occasion you will want to vary this procedure by having them help you retell it or by asking one of them to do it. This book lends itself to another procedure. Here the visions are retold in a form which lends itself to a dramatic reading by the class much in the manner that is done by speech choirs. There is the "director," the "narrator," and the various characters. You will find this procedure effective as an addition to the method suggested above.

3. "What does the text say?" Be sure to have the class members document by reference to the text their statement about what the text

says. Careful attention to this procedure will save you and the class many a pitfall, controversy, or fruitless debate. The sections in each chapter entitled "Interpretation" will guide you in this process.

4. The climax of the lesson comes when you state the message of the vision. First consider the message for the seven churches of Asia who were facing serious internal problems and external opposition and even persecution from the society and the political structures around them. Then ask, "What does it say to you personally? What difference would it make if you took this seriously?"

The Format of the Chapters of This Book

With some modifications depending on the nature of the content, each chapter will include introduction, vision, interpretation, and message.

1. Introduction

The purpose of the introduction is to set the stage for seeing the vision which follows. On occasion the setting is given. Again, the content of the vision may be outlined briefly, or the importance of the vision in the framework of the entire book may be emphasized. In each case the purpose is to provide sufficient orientation for the reader so that he can proceed to the vision itself.

2. Vision (You are there!)

To assist the reader in the process of visualization the vision is retold. This is not a translation or a paraphrase but a dramatic retelling of the vision.

3. Interpretation

In an effort to avoid isogesis, that is, reading one's own ideas or wishes into the text, the stress in this section is on "What does the text say?"

4. Message

The attempt here is to state the meaning of the text for its readers.

Class Discussion Questions From "Visions of Glory"

Chapter 1. What were your impressions the first time you read Revelation? From what sources have you gotten most of your information about the interpretation of the book?

Chapter 2. How does the vision of the Glorified Christ compare with your normal mental pictures of Christ? What accounts for the difference?

Chapter 3. Perhaps you would like to compose a letter to your congregation on the model of John's letters.

Chapter 4. Our cry to God, contrary to 6:9-10 is more for mercy than for retribution. Are there Christians in the world today who can identify themselves more with these verses? Why is there such a difference? Where is our responsibility in this difference?

Chapter 5. Do you have difficulties in believing that God's will lies behind all the tragedies of history?

Chapter 6. In what ways is the life story of the two witnesses intended to be a model for Christians today? What differences would it make in our life style if we followed their model?

Chapter 7. Are there any ways in which John's criticisms of Rome are valid for our society today? How do you suppose people of his day responded to criticisms of their country?

Chapter 8. The chapter refers to the "law of the harvest." If there is a judgment against our society, to what degree is that also a judgment against us?

Chapter 9. Can the teaching of the wrath of God be meaningful to our generation? How can it be balanced with the love of God?

Chapter 10. Many commentators predict the collapse of our society by the year 2000 A.D. If the visions of the fall of Babylon would also apply to our own time in a literal way, what would your response be?

Chapter 11. This chapter speaks of final triumph and celebration. Knowing that Heaven will triumph someday, to what degree do we need to right injustices which exist now?

Chapter 12. Looking back over the book of Revelation, what are some ways to incorporate its message into your living? What personal response have you made to its visions of the loving Christ?

Chapter 13. Compare your feelings about the book of Revelation with those you had when first reading it. What has made the changes? Has the study of Revelation affected your understanding of today's history?

1
The Problem and the Glory

Revelation has caused more trouble for pastors and congregations than any other book in the Bible. At the same time it is the most neglected and least read. Many have taken it up to read, only to lay it down bewildered by its grotesque images and incomprehensible visions. Others confessing "fear" and "very much unease" with Revelation are hesitant even to pick it up. One student confessed, "I had all but tossed the book out" before taking a class in Revelation. In having this feeling he was in good company with two great leaders of the Protestant Reformation, Luther and Zwingli. Luther wanted to deny a place in the canon of Scripture to Revelation and declared that such images and visions are found no place else in the Bible. The Swiss reformer, Zwingli, was equally vehement: "With the Apocalypse (that is, Revelation) we have no concern for it is not a biblical book."

At the same time Revelation possesses the strange fascination of the unknown and the mysterious, of promises to unveil the future. Over ten million Americans have succumbed to the allure of Hal Lindsey's *The Late Great Planet Earth*, his version of "pop-eschatology," much of which interweaves apocalyptic material from Revelation, Daniel, and other parts of the Bible. The Jehovah's Witnesses in 1972 packed thousands into a Cicero, Illinois racetrack for a four-day meeting in which a speaker predicted that 1975 would be "close to the end" of the world. For many others movies like *Omen* are fueling fires of speculation about the demonic and the antichrist.

Headlines in the *Los Angeles Times* for July 28, 1976 proclaim more sobering facts, "When the Time Came in L.A., Heavens Stayed Closed—but Prophet Carries On." The article itself tells of the prediction of a local minister that "exactly 144,000 Christians would assemble in Los Angeles on a certain April day in 1976 and would experience 'the greatest event of our generation' . . . Come April 14, 1976—the divinely ordained day— . . . the heavenly display fizzled. No parting heavens, no noisy wind, no fire." Nor did the end of the world come recently for the thirty persons who holed up in a house in Grannis, Arkansas rapturously anticipating that event.

Why is Revelation such a problem? Why has it called forth such strident "pop-eschatologies" and such vehement blasts of opposition?

For one reason, Revelation is unique among the books of the New Testament. Here we are in a strange and unfamiliar world, teeming with wierd and grotesque images and symbols impossible to depict save with the heightened imagination. Read the first five verses of chapter seventeen. Is it any wonder that the average reader in the twentieth century throws up his hands in defeat when confronted by a book so strange and different from the other books of the New Testament?

Revelation is also a problem because it has been misused. Perhaps the most serious misuse is that Revelation has been made into a time-table of history. A book published in 1941 for example and running through three editions by 1947 prints a chart of the ages. According to the chart the 7th bowl of wrath was to end in the 1940's and presumably the great battle of Armageddon would follow. In the same volume the spirit of evil was seen to have its political manifestation in the actions of Mussolini. The whore sitting upon the waters was identified as the Catholic Church.

Throughout the history of the Christian church individuals in every generation have attempted on the basis of Revelation to chart the chronological course of history—*and everyone of them has been dead wrong*.

Revelation is a problem, finally, because it has been neglected. The strange character of Revelation as well as its misuse has led to the disuse of Revelation by many Christians. Apart from the Christ's invitation in the twentieth verse of the third chapter, "Behold, I stand at the door and knock; if anyone hears my voice and opens the door, I will come in to him and eat with him, and he with me," and the colorful pictures of the New Jerusalem, the New Heaven, and the New Earth at the end of the book, for most Christians Revelation is a sealed book. Even most students in theological seminary have had almost no acquaintance with the book.

The Importance of the Book of Revelation

Although it has been called the most difficult book in the Bible to interpret it is inestimably worthwhile to do so—not only because of the havoc wrought in congregations by its misuse but more because we come in touch with the life and death struggles of the early Christian communities. We see their faithfulness as well as their apostacy, their loyalty as well as their too easy tolerance, their "little power" and self-deception. But above all, blazing in the face of martyrdom, glows their faith that Christ risen from the dead has conquered. Beyond the machinations of men, God is still on the throne and those who are faithful unto death will receive the crown of life and will not be hurt by the second death. "He shall reign forever and ever! Hallelujah!"

Features That Have Made Revelation a Problem

1. In Revelation we are confronted by an *ancient world view*. The stage for the drama of Revelation is a three-storied universe. The drama of Revelation is enacted in Heaven before the throne of God, on earth in the midst of humanity, and under the earth (5:3). This simply will not do for the modern mind. We can no longer think of God as out there or up there in space. Transcendence in that sense is gone. The Copernican revolution has seen to that. It is no longer possible to view the earth as a flat square with four corners (7:1). Our astronauts who have circled the globe in ninety minutes have knocked that idea into a cocked hat.

2. In the second place we are confronted by an *ancient timetable*. John the Revelator expected the end of history to come in his own day. Again and again he says that he is depicting what is to take place *soon* (1:1, 3; 6:10-11; 22:6, 20). By no stretch of the imagination can "soon" be stretched to cover two thousand years.

3. In the third place in Revelation we are confronted by *ancient imagery*. The grotesque, unnatural, and impossible imagery of the apocalypse is strange to contemporary experience and is unreal to us. In chapter 12 for instance we see a great red dragon with seven heads and ten horns, who with one swoop of his tail casts one-third of the stars down to earth. This, the modern mind cannot accept as literal. Astronomers tell us that there are about 30 billion stars that they can photograph. The average star is about 865,000 miles through and the dwarf stars about 25,000 miles in diameter. Just imagine if you can one-third of the stars, that is, some 10 billion stars each one of them vastly larger than the earth being swept by the tail of the dragon on to this little pin point of a globe on which we live. Incredible! Dragons with 7 heads, locusts with women's hair and lion's teeth simply do not exist in any material sense (cf. 9:7 f).

4. Much of this imagery is conveyed in *visions*. We children of the 20th century are afraid of visions. Psychology has made us feel that

people who have visions belong in a mental institution. So when we read of John's visions on the isle of Patmos, we almost instinctively conclude that his imprisonment and anguish of spirit have made him mad. Thus visions per se present a problem for us.

5. In the fifth place we are confronted in the Book of Revelation by *ancient mysteries*, i.e., by mysteries that are of a different character, that belong to a different age from ours: a scroll sealed with seven seals (5:1), the mystery of the seven thunders (10:4), twenty-four elders sitting on thrones and casting down their golden crowns before the throne of God (ch. 4), a beast that was and is not, and is an eighth but belongs to the seven (ch. 17), mysterious numbers such as "a time, times, and a half a time," 3½ years and 666.

6. In the sixth place we are confronted in the Book of Revelation with a view of God that seems other than the God of our Lord Jesus Christ. The loving Father seems to have given way to the wrathful Pantokrator, the Almighty, the all-terrible God. Chapter 1 verse 8 reads, "'I am the Alpha and the Omega,' says the Lord God, who is and who was and who is to come, the Almighty." When the 6th seal is opened, children of the earth cry out to be hidden from the wrath of him who sits on the throne. The martyred saints under the altar in chapter 6 cry out, "How long, O Lord, before thou wilt judge and avenge our blood on those who dwell on the earth?" But perhaps most dramatic of all is the reaping by the angel who has the sharp sickle of the grape harvest. He throws the vintage of the earth into the great wine press of the wrath of God. The wine press is trodden outside the city. Blood flows from the wine press, as high as a horse's bridle, for about two hundred miles (ch. 14). This is not a book for weak stomachs or sentimentalists.

7. Coupled with this picture of God we are confronted with a Christ who has a sharp two-edged sword sticking out of his mouth and is called the Lion of the tribe of Judah. In chapter 14 we see him reaping the earth with a sharp sickle. In 19 we see him as commander of the armies of heaven, riding a white horse, judging and making war. With the sharp two-edged sword sticking out of his mouth he smites the nations, rules them with a rod of iron, and treads the wine press of the fury of the wrath of God the Pantokrator. All this seems a far cry from the gentle Jesus, meek and mild, and friend of sinners as seen in the Gospels.

These then are the major problems presented to us by Revelation: 1. A 3-storied, un-scientific universe. 2. An ancient timetable for history. 3. Fantastic, unbelievable imagery. 4. Weird impossible visions.

5. Unintelligible mysteries. 6. A seemingly non-Christian view of God. 7. A seemingly different Christ from the friend of sinners of the Gospels.

We turn now to view the glory of the book of Revelation. In the familiar Sistine Chapel in Rome are fresco masterpieces painted by some of the greatest artists of all time. Here in massive murals is depicted the entire history of mankind. We begin with the ceiling where Michaelangelo with moving power has caught the very moment of creation. The side panels depict on the left scenes from the Old Testament and on the right their fulfillment in the New. The whole course of history flows to its fulfillment in the gigantic fresco behind the altar. There stands one thing which the pious worshiper cannot help seeing. As Burkitt[1] well says: "He cannot raise his eyes to adore the consecrated Host without being confronted with the Last Judgment. Behind the Priest, behind the altar, behind the lighted candles, behind the sacred drama of worship, the Last Judgment is always there. . . . The Pope's Chapel . . . faithfully reflects the Christian scheme of things: behind everything the Last Judgment looms in the background, universal, inevitable." This is "the divine event towards which all nature moves." Burkitt holds that the Last Judgment is the divine event towards which Revelation and all apocalypses move.

In this he is mistaken for he has missed the last two chapters of Revelation. The glory of Revelation is not the last judgment. The glory of Revelation is the New Heaven and the New Earth; it is the New Jerusalem coming down out of heaven adorned as a bride for her husband; it is God making all things *new;* it is God dwelling with us, wiping away every tear; it is death replaced by the water of *life* given without money and without price; it is to live in the continual presence of God and the Lamb as son or daughter; it is to fulfill our chief end: "to glorify God and enjoy him forever!"

Four Keys to Interpreting the Book of Revelation

What keys have been proposed to unlock the riddle of Revelation? The methods of interpretation commonly suggested may be gathered into four and dubbed: 1. The Timeless Look, 2. The Forward Look, 3. The Sweeping Look, and 4. The Backward Look.

1. *The Timeless Look* is called by various names: "the timeless symbolism" interpretation, "the idealist or spiritualist" view, or in contemporary theological jargon, "the demythologizing" interpretation. This view holds that the author uses traditional apocalyptic symbolism and mythological imagery to convey eternal truth. The symbols are not in-

tended to be taken literally. The author has no concrete historical situation in mind. To find the hidden truth we must demythologize the symbols and thus arrive at truth that can be understood by twentieth century man.

2. *The Forward Look.* Others call it "the futurist" interpretation. The Germans call it *endgeschichtlich,* (end historical) or eschatological, since it deals with the time of the *eschaton,* the end of history. By these designations the proponents of the forward look are trying to say that from chapter 6 on, if not from chapter 4, Revelation deals with events that will occur in the time of the end. The extreme futurists would hold that even the first three chapters belong to the end-time, even though they are addressed to "the seven churches that are in Asia."

3. *The Sweeping Look* is known to the Germans as the *kirchengeschichtlich* (church historical) or the *weltgeschichtlich* (world historical) and to others as the "continuous-historical." By this school of interpreters, Revelation is thought to describe the history of the world or of the church from the writer's day on to the end of history. To put it another way, they would hold that the entire sweep of history lies hidden in the mysteries of Revelation. In unlocking the mysteries of Revelation we find the key to the course of events in our own time; in fact, we open the door of understanding to the panorama of all ages. Howard B. Rand for example, is brash enough to give dates for the period covered by each of the seals: The First Seal—31 B.C. to 64 A.D. . . . The Second Seal—64 to 313 A.D. . . . The Sixth Seal—1755-96 A.D. to 194-?[2] Even Mr. Rand was not brash enough to name the exact year for the ending of the sixth seal.

A recent writer has appropriately called such interpretations "pop-eschatology."[3] Another has dubbed the attempt to make Revelation into a calendar of events in world history the "calendarizing" view.[4]

There have been calendarizers throughout Christian history who have set dates and even given away their possessions in anticipation of being "raptured" to Heaven. They have all been wrong! Most calendarizers of today are a bit more cautious. Yet they still fervently believe and proclaim as did every calendarizer of Christian history that the events taking place *now* are the fulfillment of Biblical prophecy.

True, the New Testament church did have a vivid sense of expectancy of the return of Christ. This was caught up in admonitions such as "Watch!" "Pray!" "Be ready!" But these exhortations were tempered by the realization that "of that day and hour no one knows, not even the angels of heaven, nor the Son, but the Father only." (Mt. 24:36)

4. *The Backward Look*, commonly known as the "preterist" view. The preterist holds that the prophecies of Revelation have been fulfilled in the past, i.e., in the author's own day. Consequently, the Germans call this view *zeitgeschichtlich*, (contemporary-historical). The End was at hand in his day. However, The New Heaven and New Earth has not come, The Kingdom of God is still to be consummated.

None of these four views is sufficient in itself. The timeless view neglects both the concrete, historical crisis out of which Revelation arose and to which it spoke as well as the reality of the consummation of history that is coming in the future. The forward view, while overemphasizing the future, neglects the past. The "sweeping look" twists Revelation to conform to the course of history and especially to the events of one's own time. The "backward look" in overemphasizing the past may tend to overlook the importance of Revelation for our day and the consummation of all things coming in the future.

Amid all these problems and conflicting views, how can the minister or layman find his way out of the gathering storm thundering in the wild wilderness of the Apocalypse of John?

Many years ago a Bible teacher came to Professor E. B. Hoff confessing that Revelation was an enigma to him and asking what Hoff himself believed about the book. Hoff was a wise teacher. He told the man, "Go and read what the book itself says and come back and we'll talk." On the second visit Hoff asked, "What did the book say?" And on hearing the reply, E. B. Hoff said, "That's what I believe." And so it went all through the book of Revelation.

When this writer heard this story, he studied Revelation in the same way, without neglecting the writings of scholars. This has been the basic key for unlocking the book for him. What does the book say about itself? What is the author trying to say to the readers by this passage? Look at the book itself. The question, "What does the text say?" will constantly recur in each chapter.

Study shows Revelation to be related to three types of literature: letter, apocalypse, and prophecy. Recognizing these types leads to a number of principles of interpretation.

Revelation as a Letter

The first principle of interpretation is as follows: *Read Revelation as a letter to the church of the first century and specifically to the churches of the province of Asia.*

Revelation 1:4 reads, "John to the seven churches that are in Asia:

Grace to you and peace . . . " In verse 11 the churches are named: Ephesus, Smyrna, Pergamum, Thyatira, Sardis, Philadelphia, and Laodicea. The author states that he is writing a letter to a group of churches in the province of Asia. So, to understand what the book of Revelation has to say, find out what it had to say to the readers for whom the author wrote the book, i.e., the members of the churches of his day.

Second, there is no better way to try to understand Revelation than for a person to place himself through the use of imagination, in the position of a member of one of the seven churches to whom John writes.

The imagination is one of God's finest gifts. By use of the imagination a person is able to transcend the limits of one's own situation in time and space and imaginatively enter into the thoughts and feelings of persons of other times and places. One can, through imagination, "walk in the moccasins of another" and to an important extent, see through the eyes of the other person. It is the supreme gift of the creative artist, poet, and actor to light the fires of our imagination so that we can vicariously enter into the truth embodied in the painting, the poem, or the play. When this happens, then we understand not merely with the head, but also with the heart. The second principle in interpreting Revelation is to *place yourself imaginatively in one of the churches of the province of Asia*.

Revelation is a message to Christians facing possible persecution, imprisonment, and martyrdom. Chapters 2 and 3 specifically relate problems of apathy, compromise, and false teaching within the congregations. However, the most serious threat to the church's existence was persecution without. The Christians of Asia Minor were being persecuted by Roman officials for refusing to worship the emperor and the goddess, Roma. John himself is on the rocky island of Patmos sharing their tribulation, because of his Christian witness. Origen says, "The Roman Emperor . . . condemned John to the island of Patmos for witnessing to the word of truth."

Verse 13 of chapter 2 documents further the persecution that faced the church. One member, Antipas, has already suffered martyrdom. Revelation 2:10 reads "Do not fear what you are about to suffer. Behold, the devil is about to throw some of you into prison that you may be tested. . . . Be faithful unto death and I will give you the crown of life." In the fifth seal of chapter 6 we see martyrs under the altar.

The third principle is to *read Revelation as a message to Christians facing persecution, imprisonment, and possible martyrdom*.

John now and then plainly tells his readers what the point of the book is. For example, Revelation 13:10 reads, "Here is a call for the endurance and the faith of the saints." Could any statement of purpose be clearer? The fourth principle of interpretation thus is: *Look for places where the author plainly tells you what the message is.*

The first four principles are: 1. Read Revelation as a letter to the seven churches of Asia. 2. Place yourself as a member in one of the seven churches. 3. Read it as a message to Christians facing persecution and possible martyrdom. 4. Note the places where the author tells you plainly what his message is. These four principles grow out of the nature of Revelation as a letter.

Revelation Is Also an Apocalypse

The very first verse of the book tells us that it is a "revelation" even though it differs in important ways from typical apocalypses. What is a "revelation"? Here is the source of much present-day misunderstanding of Revelation, for most people do not know what an apocalypse is. Revelation is the only New Testament book that belongs to apocalyptic literature. Apocalyptic literature developed during the exilic and post-exilic periods in Judaism out of crisis situations confronted by the Jewish people. Their land was under the heel of foreign power. They were under the domination of Gentiles. They were suffering persecution. Yet, they believed that they were the chosen people of God. How could these two opposites be reconciled? The apocalyptic writers accomplished this by the doctrine of two ages: the present age of suffering is under the domination of satanic powers and is doomed to destruction; the future age is the golden age when God will reward his people by making all things new and punishing the demonic forces of evil. Then, as William Barclay so well puts it, "God Himself would descend into the arena of events; God Himself would come striding onto the stage of history; He would blast this present world out of existence, and bring in His own golden time."[5]

Revelation differs from typical Jewish apocalypses in these notable ways: It includes a body of seven letters. It was written by John using his own name rather than the name of some ancient well-known person. Jesus and Christian symbolism are introduced. Instead of the thoroughgoing pessimism about the present, Revelation expresses John's hope and optimism based on what Jesus accomplished in history in the past and his present presence amidst the churches as well as on God's coming intervention to set up His kingdom in the future.

The only way in which this idea of history could be portrayed — since events had not yet occurred — was in dramatic pictures, in
visions and symbols. The eternal verities of heaven had to be depicted in
human terms. Spiritual truth had to be conveyed in material symbols — such as golden streets and pearly gates.

The fact that Revelation is an apocalypse suggests the following ad-
ditional principles of interpretation:

Fifth, read it for its religious values. Revelation is a religious and
not a scientific book. This becomes apparent when we begin to look
carefully at the dramatic pictures John paints. Take the vision of the
sixth seal in chapter 6. Here not only do the stars fall to earth but in the
same vision, the sky vanishes like a scroll that is rolled up. It is like a
gigantic window blind — when the tension is released it snaps together
and vanishes "into thin air." And yet in chapter 8 and elsewhere, the sky
and the stars are back again. Or is there anyone who really believes that
Christ has an actual sword sticking out of his mouth as he is portrayed in
chapter 1? Revelation is not a scientific book. In it, as a rule, two plus
two do not equal four. They equal five, nine, or eleven — anything other
than four. So the fifth principle of interpretation is: *Read Revelation for its religious values.* Do not expect it to give scientific
information.

Then, since Revelation is a book of apocalyptic visions, see the visions with your imagination. Read it aloud as a grand opera which has
the universe as its stage. Here is a great religious drama staged in
heaven, on earth, and under the earth — the whole universe is the stage.
With your imagination guided by the details of the text, get the picture.
See it in your mind's eye, and your heart will be moved by its power.
The sixth principle of interpretation is this: *Read Revelation aloud. See
the visions with your imagination controlled by the text.*

The seventh principle is a corollary of the sixth. *Most of the details
of a vision have no special meaning apart from their contribution to the
total vision.* The white hair of chapter one is probably there because of a
literary relationship to Daniel 7:9 where God is so pictured. Thus it has
no special meaning of its own apart from its contribution to the total
picture of the glorified Christ.

Revelation Is Also a Prophecy

Many have a very false idea of what a prophet is. In popular understanding, a prophet is one who foretells the future. So people speak of
"weather prophets" who tell what the weather is going to be like tomor-

row or for the next five days or the next month. The biblical prophet is fundamentally a spokesman for God, an enthusiast for Yahweh who brings God's message to the people of his own day. His concern is for his own people in his own day. His feet are rooted in his own time. Prediction is basically for the purpose of bringing the people of his day back to God.

It has been aptly said that biblical prophecy is two-dimensional, having height and breadth but with little concern for depth, i.e., chronology of future events.[6] The prophet blends the near and the distant. It is as if he were looking at a range of mountains. He sees some of the peaks but not the intervening hills and valleys. The future and the ultimate is viewed as imminent. Every generation can live with a sense of urgency and expectancy for God who himself is ultimate has spoken his word.

Revelation 19:10 provides an insight into how John thought of a prophet. "The testimony of Jesus is the spirit of prophecy." Testimony means "witness." A prophet thus is one who bears witness to Jesus either by giving his life as a martyr or by word of mouth and deed. In claiming Revelation to be a prophecy, John is in effect saying, "This is an inspired book because it contains a message from God to my people."

The eighth principle of interpretation is: *Look for the eternal and timeless message of God in John's message for the people of his day.*

In summary, eight principles of interpretation which grow out of the nature of Revelation as a letter, an apocalypse, and a prophecy are these:

1. Read Revelation as a letter to the church of the first century and specifically to the churches of the province of Asia.
2. Place yourself as a member of one of the seven churches of Asia.
3. Read Revelation as a message to Christians facing possible martyrdom.
4. Look for places where the author plainly tells you what the message is.
5. Read Revelation for its religious values. Do not expect it to give you scientific information.
6. See the visions by using your controlled imagination.
7. Remember that most of the details have no special meaning apart from their contribution to the total vision.
8. Look for the eternal and timeless measure of God in John's message for the people of his day.

1. Burkitt, F. Crawford, *Jewish and Christian Apocalypses*. Oxford University Press, 1914, p. 2.
2. Rand, Howard B., *Study in Revelation*. Destiny, 1941, pp. 36, 39, 53.
3. Marty, Martin, review of Lindsey, Hal, "Satan Is Alive and Well on Planet Earth," *Critic*, Vol. 31:84 (Mar-Apr) 1973, p. 80.
4. Eller, Vernard, *The Most Revealing Book of the Bible: Making Sense Out of Revelation*. Eerdman, 1974, Chapter 1.
5. Barclay, William, *The Revelation of John*. Westminster, 1977, p. 4.
6. Ladd, George E., *Commentary on the Revelation of John*, Eerdman, 1971, p. 22.

2
The Glorified Christ
1:1-20

Introduction

Books of the first century A.D. were usually written in scroll form on papyrus thinly cut from a reedy plant common in the Middle East especially in the Nile valley of Egypt. Our word, paper, is derived from the term, papyrus. In all probability, the handwritten original of our book of Revelation was penned by John on a papyrus scroll. Normally information about title and author was written at the end, i.e., on the inside of the scroll. However, in order for the reader to become informed earlier about those matters, the practice arose of giving this information at the beginning. So John begins with the title, the writer, and the blessing.

Text 1:1-3

The revelation from Jesus Christ which God gave to him to show to his slaves what must soon take place. He made it known by sending his messenger to his slave John, who by telling what he saw testified to the saving purpose of God and the confirming testimony of Jesus Christ.

Blessed is he who reads aloud the words of this prophecy and those who hear and obey the things written in it for the time is near.

Interpretation: What does the text say?

Revelation is not used in verse 1 as the technical term scholars employ to refer to the body of Jewish and Christian writing characterized by the "apocalyptic" pattern of thought. Here it means the supernatural disclosure of divine truths especially those truths connected with the fulfillment of the Kingdom of God in the end-time.

At the same time the Book of Revelation does belong to the class of literature called by scholars apocalypses. Apocalyptic thought despaired of history and confidently looked to God to decisively intervene in the very near future to annihilate the powers of evil, save his faithful remnant, and set up his eternal kingdom. In apocalypses, this plan of God is revealed in dreams, fantastic visions, and grotesque imagery.

Revelation differs from Jewish apocalypses in several notable ways. Jesus and Christian symbolism are introduced. His death in history is central in God's plan of redemption. While Jewish apocalypses are pseudonymous, John, the author, is known to his readers. Further, the book contains seven letters written to churches in Asia Minor. In fact, Revelation as a whole may be considered to be an apocalypse written within the framework of a letter.

The original title of the book was not "The Revelation to John" as in the Revised Standard Version nor was it "The Revelation of St. John the Divine" as the melodious King James would have it. Neither of these is earlier than the fourth century A.D. It was "The Revelation of Jesus Christ." The first words of the superscription are in all probability the original title of the book.

The title may be taken in two ways. Some scholars hold that Jesus Christ is the content of the revelation. It is more likely, however, that **of Jesus Christ** in this passage refers to the fact that Jesus Christ is the one through whom the disclosure of "what must soon take place" came to John. God gave the revelation to Jesus Christ, who made it known by sending his angel-messenger to his slave, John. John makes it known to Christ's slaves through his scroll. He intends the scroll to be read aloud to the expectant congregation by the liturgist in the worship service on the Lord's Day. John is detained on Patmos and cannot speak as a prophet in their presence. He expects the worshipers to receive his words as an "inspired message," i.e., prophecy. The saving message comes from God himself and bears the confirming testimony of Jesus Christ. Accordingly, the liturgist who reads Revelation aloud and the worshipers who hear and obey its admonitions are divinely blessed. At the end of the reading of the scroll the worshipers hear the same admonition and the same promise of eternal blessing reinforced by solemn warnings (22:6-19).

The translation of the Greek word *doulos* as "servant" is largely limited to Bible translations. It is a misleading "watering-down" of the original meaning. *Doulos* means "slave." The economy of the ancient world was built on the foundation of slavery. Athens in the time of Demetrius Phalerus had four hundred thousand slaves to twenty thousand free citizens. Caesar sold sixty-three thousand Gauls into slavery on one occasion. Gibbon estimates that the slave and free population in Rome were equal in the time of Claudius.

Paul frequently refers to himself as a "slave of Christ" (cf. Romans 1:1; Galatians 1:10; Philippians 1:1), i.e., subject to Christ, owned by him—soul and body, so much so that Paul could say, "No longer I live, but Christ lives in me." It is in this sense of complete dedication and obedience to God and Christ that John speaks of himself, his fellow "prophets" and his fellow Christians as "slaves."

The two key phrases of the superscription are "the word" of God, i.e., the saving purpose of God,[1] and the testimony of Jesus. The two Greek words are *logos* and *marturia*. *Logos* can mean word, thought, message, action, deed, plan, wisdom, cause, and much more. Central to the Biblical idea of the word of God is dynamic, creative activity. God said, "Let there be light." And light came into existence. The only weapon the conquering Christ of Revelation has is the sharp sword sticking out his mouth, i.e., his Word. *Marturia* means witness, attestation, confirmation, verification, validation, and especially in later Greek, martyrdom. It is possible here that *marturia* may have a double connotation. It can mean confirmation by Jesus of what God has done, is doing, and is about to do. At the same time, that confirmation is made by Jesus, the "Protomartyr," who attested to the saving purpose of God by being crucified, i.e., by being martyred.

The two phrases, "the word of God" and "the testimony of Jesus" are in apposition to what he saw. By this John is not merely attesting to the fact that he saw the visions. He means that what he saw has the character of being active and certain. It is God's plan of salvation and judgment. It is God who brings it to pass. It is Christ who confirms God's action by his word, deed, death, and resurrection. In a real sense the entire book of Revelation can be summed up in those two phrases: "God's plan of salvation" and "verified by Jesus."

Apocalypses are born in crises. The urgency for action characteristic of apocalypses is seen in "what must soon take place" and "the time is near." It is of utmost importance to recognize clearly that the point of reference for John was not the twentieth century, but the end of the first, i.e., his own day. The Greek word *kairos* means "the decisive moment," "the critical time," and in Revelation it has the implication of the time of judgment, of fulfillment, the end-time. "Must" refers to the certainty of the fulfillment of God's purpose.

While John felt that the time was near, he did not set dates. He did not "calendarize." But with the early church he did live in expectancy of

Christ's return. His basic stance was that of courageous, *steadfast endurance* in the face of present and coming tribulation or suffering, so that he would become a conqueror through faith in God's promises (cf. v. 9). Three determinative points for John's theology and life were: 1. the death of Christ and the redemption he wrought for mankind; 2. the resurrected Christ's presence in the midst of the congregations; and 3. the end-time in which Christ would complete the conquest of evil and bring in the fullness of the kingdom of God.

Text 1:4-5 You are there!

(In your imagination take your place in the worship service of a Christian congregation in Asia Minor at the end of the first century. It is Sunday, the Lord's day. The congregation is assembled for worship. It has been rumored that a letter has come from the prophet John.

The leader addresses the congregation: "I have a letter from our brother John imprisoned on the isle of Patmos. He has received in a vision a revelation of our Risen Lord Jesus Christ who has commanded John to write this message to you. Listen to his letter.)

> Blessed are you who hear and who keep what is written in this letter for the time is near!
> May the gracious favor and peace of God who is, who was, and who is coming and from the Seven Spirits which are before his throne, and from Jesus Christ, the Faithful Witness, the Firstborn of the Dead, the Ruler of the kings of the earth, be yours.
> To Christ who loves us and has set us free from our sins by his death and made us into his kingdom, (we shall rule with him) priests who have free access to his God and Father, to him be the glory and the dominion for ever and ever. Amen.
> Hear this! Christ is coming with the clouds. Every eye will see him. All who have rejected him will wail and tremble with fear because of him. So be it! Amen!
> I am the Alpha and the Omega, the beginning and the end, says the Lord God who is and who was and who is coming, the Almighty.

Interpretation

Possibly under the influence of Paul's practice, John writes his message to the churches in letter form. Just as we have a standard form for our letters so did the New Testament writers. Their letter form included: a. the writer, b. the recipients, c. the greeting, d. the thanksgiving, e. the body of the letter, and f. the concluding greetings and benediction. In Revelation we have a. "John . . . b. to the seven churches . . . c. grace to you . . . d. to him be glory," then e. the body of the book, and f. the benediction, "the grace of the Lord . . . Amen."

The Writer

John must have been well known to the churches of the Roman province of Asia. He saw no need to identify himself specifically. He calls himself "a slave" of Jesus Christ (v. 2) and "your brother and co-partner" (v. 9). These terms would apply to his fellow Christians in the seven churches.

The Recipients

Note also that within the larger "letter" there is a group of seven letters to the seven churches that are in Asia. This anchors Revelation in a concrete historical context. John knows them by name (v. 11) and writes with a pastor's concern for their spiritual welfare.

There were many other churches in the province of Asia by the end of the first century A.D. We know of Colossia (Colossians 1:2), Hierapolis (Colossians 4:13) and Troas (Acts 20:5-12). Not more than twenty years later, Ignatius writes to Tralles and Magnesia. Seven is a number signifying wholeness or completeness. Here the seven symbolically represent the whole church.

Greeting

"May the unmerited favor and peace of the everlasting God, the Spirit in all his fullness, and the living, ruling Christ, the faithful martyr, be yours."

Who is, who was, and who is coming is one of John's designations for God the Father. It emphasizes the eternity as well as the presence of God in history. The sequence of tenses emphasizes the present and the future. The God of the past is active now. This will climax in his coming in fullness in the future when his purpose is completely worked out (cf. chs. 21-22). In a similar way Christ is present among the churches now (1:9-20) and is coming (1:7). **The Seven Spirits** is John's way of designating the fullness and completeness of the Holy Spirit.

The Christian knows that Christ, not Caesar, is the real **ruler of the kings of the earth**.

Thanksgiving
    The love and redemptive work of Christ is lifted up in the doxology. A common New Testament affirmation is that Christians will rule with Christ and perform the functions of worship. They have direct access to God. They need no priest. Perhaps this also means that they may share in his redemptive work. This doxology is addressed to Christ rather than to God.

The Message
    What Christians see with the eye of faith will be visible to all peoples. Christ is coming as victor, ruler, and judge. All who have had a part in rejecting him will wail in expectation of their coming judgment.

The Attestation
    Alpha and *Omega* are the beginning and the ending letters of the Greek alphabet. Here they are used as a symbol for God who controls the beginning and the end and all that happens in between. He is the All-powerful Ruler, the Eternal. He is coming, i.e., God will bring history to its divinely determined consummation.

THE VISION OF THE GLORIFIED CHRIST   1:9-20

Introduction
    The importance of the initial vision in chapters 1-3 of the Glorified Christ walking in the midst of the churches cannot be overemphasized. It has a significant message for the church. In addition, it has important "imprint" value for the remainder of Revelation. All of the visions of the Apocalypse of John must be seen against the overarching background of the victorious, resurrected, regal, glorified Messiah, who has now taken a firm hold on the reins of the universe and has begun to rule.
    The setting is the rocky volcanic island of Patmos off the coast of Asia Minor some sixty miles southwest of Ephesus. With his fellow Christians, John has suffered persecution. He met suffering with courageous patience and endurance for the sake of the kingdom. Now because he had preached God's plan of salvation and testified to Jesus he was banished to Patmos. Perhaps he was sentenced to hard labor in the quarries there.
    In the vision which follows, how large is the figure of Christ? How large would he have to be to hold seven stars in his right hand? Or to have a voice as loud as a trumpet, or as the roar of the sea? Or to cause

John to fall down as though dead? Gigantic proportions are required to depict this royal, high-priestly vision of Christ.

The visions of Revelation take place on the stage of the universe. No puny stage this! The interpreter needs to free the powers of his imagination and let the text itself determine the majesty of each vision.

The Vision
YOU ARE THERE

Look!	It is very early Sunday morning on the rocky island of Patmos. Banished to that penal colony, John the prophet is already at work in the quarries.	
	Caught up by the Spirit he meditates.	
	The sun rises across the sea.	
	"It's the day of our resurrected Lord, not Caesar's!"	
Listen!	Suddenly behind him a loud voice blares like a trumpet, *What you see, write in a book and send it to the seven churches: to Ephesus, Smyrna, Pergamum, Thyatira, Sardis, Philadelphia, and Laodicea!*	1:10 11
Look!	Turning to see the imperial voice speaking to him, John sees seven huge golden candelabra and standing in their midst the gigantic, imposing regal Son of Man . . . clothed in a robe reaching down to his feet with a golden scarf around his shoulders.	12 13
	His head and hair are pure white, like snow.	14
	His eyes flame like fire.	
	His feet shine as burnished, refined brass.	15
Listen!	His voice sounds like the surf of the sea pounding upon the rocks of Patmos Isle.	
Look!	In his right hand extending to the sky he holds seven stars	16
	Out of his mouth comes a sharp two-edged sword	

His face blazes like the sun at high
noon.

See!   John swoons from fright.   17
Look! Listen! The Son of Man reaches down and
touches him with his right hand
and says,
Don't be afraid!
I am the First and the Last and the Liv-   18
ing One!
I was dead, but see! I am alive forever-
more!
And I hold the keys to Death and to
Hades!
Write what you see,   19
what is present and
what is to come in the future.
The secret of the seven stars that you   20
saw in my right hand and of the
seven golden candelabra is this:
the seven stars are the angels of the
seven churches, and the seven
candelabra are the seven churches.

Interpretation: What does the text say?

The central figure in this vision is called, **one like a son of man,** (v. 13), **the first and the last** (v. 17), **the living one** who died but now is alive forever and possesses the **keys of Death and Hades.** Christian hearers would understand **son of man** to be a messianic designation. For them the one who died and is now risen could be none other than Jesus Christ.

The details of the vision create an overwhelming sense of the royal splendor and ruling power of the living Christ. His bearing and garb are regal and high priestly. The high priest's "girdle" seems to have been a loosely woven scarf. His eyes flame; his feet are strong as burnished brass; his voice is like the sound of many waters; his face, like the sun shining at high noon. He holds seven stars in his right hand and out of his mouth issues a sharp two-edged sword, probably to be understood as the Word of God as in Ephesians 6:17. See also Hebrews 4:12 where God's word is invincible in achieving his purpose.

The text interprets the seven stars as angels of the seven churches and the seven lampstands as the seven churches of Asia Minor— Ephesus, Smyrna, Pergamum, Thyatira, Sardis, Philadelphia, and

Laodicea (v. 11). John may have thought that each church had its angelic representative in heaven.

All the above provides the authoritative setting for the letters which John is commanded to write to the seven churches in chapters 2 and 3.

Message

To the Christians of his day facing persecution and possible martyrdom, John proclaims the living presence of the resurrected, glorified Lord. Jesus faced persecution and death and rose victorious over them. Now he has power over death and the grave. He is in the midst of the churches as God's living presence and power.

The vision of their risen, victorious, ruling Lord provides the needed spiritual comfort, strength, and *steadfast endurance* for the terrifying visions to follow. With the experience of Christ's presence among them, visions of earthquakes, stars falling from heaven, the battle of Armageddon, and the last judgment lost their terror. Those who have the "eyes of faith" know that Christ even now rules. He has conquered, he is conquering, he will conquer! His kingdom will come on earth and be manifest to all!

---

1. I have adopted Paul S. Minear's helpful translation of the Greek word *logos* as God's saving purpose. *I Saw a New Earth,* Corpus Publications, 1969, p. 4.

3

Letters to the Seven Churches

2:1—3:22

Introduction

The vision of the Glorified Christ in the midst of the churches includes the letters to seven churches in the province of Asia. The letters themselves are not visions but messages set in a vision framework. The framework is that of the Glorified Christ dictating to John.

The unity and rhythmic structure of chapters 2 and 3 is characterized by a sevenfold pattern repeated for each of the churches.

1. Instructions to John (the address)
2. Identification of the Speaker
3. The Speaker's Knowledge
4. The Speaker's Criticisms
5. The Commands to Individual Congregations
6. The Command to All
7. The Promises

1. The Address

The churches are named for the city in which they are located. *Ephesus* was "the crowning glory and chief city" of the province of Asia. A seaport located at the mouth of the Cayster River valley, commerce from the far flung parts of the Roman Empire flowed through its portals. It was the western terminus of three great Roman roads: the great way from the east from Mesopotamia by way of Colosse and Laodicea, the road from Galatia by way of Sardis, and the highway near the Aegean coast connecting the Meander and Cayster valleys.

The chief claim of Ephesus to fame however was religious. Ephesus prided itself on being "Temple Keeper" of the temple of Diana, one of the seven wonders of the world. The Greeks commonly held that "the sun saw nothing finer in his course than Diana's temple." Its size was about 425 feet by 220 feet. One hundred twenty-seven pillars of parian marble, each pillar the gift of a king, towered sixty feet high. Thirty-six of them were overlaid with gold, jewels, and carvings. In 29 B.C. part of the temple precinct was dedicated to the worship of the Emperor and of the goddess Roma.

Founded as the result of Paul's missionary work and the efforts of Acquila and Priscilla, the church of Ephesus became the most important congregation in the province and the literary center of early Christianity.

Smyrna lies some thirty-five miles north of Ephesus at the head of the Hermes valley. Its spectacular location on a magnificent harbor dominated by Mount Pagos gives credence to Smyrna's claim to be "the glory of Asia." "The crown of Smyrna" was a familiar phrase.

As early as 195 B.C. Smyrna championed the cause of Rome and built a temple to the goddess Roma. In 26 A.D. of eleven contending cities, Smyrna alone was given the right to build a temple to the Emperor Tiberius. The city became one of the great centers of emperor worship.

Here in 155 or 156 A.D. at the instigation of Gentiles and the large Jewish population, Polycarp, bishop of Smyrna, was martyred. "Eighty and six years," he said, "I have served Christ and he has never done me wrong. How can I blaspheme my King who saved me?"

Pergamum is some fifty miles north of Smyrna and about fifteen miles from the sea. Bequeathed by her last King, Attalus III, to Rome, Pergamum became capital of the province of Asia. It was the great syncretistic pagan religious center of the province. The thousand foot high acropolis was dotted with temples to pagan deities. Among them was the huge altar to Zeus which overlooked the city and the cult of Demeter in which women had a special interest. Former kings were worshiped in the Heroon sanctuary. This was extremely fertile ground, therefore, for emperor worship of which Pergamum became the chief seat. The Asclepion on the southwest of the city was the second most famous healing center in the ancient world.

Thyatira was founded originally as a military colony on the road between Pergamum and Sardis. It is known chiefly as a trade town. Here there were numerous trade guilds including the guild of the bronze-smelters and the Red Purple Cloth Guild which had a representative in Philippi (Acts 16:14). The guilds held common meals in which food sacrificed to idols would be eaten. On the city's coins Apollo is depicted grasping the hand of the Roman emperor, suggesting that the emperor belonged in the company of the gods.

Some thirty-five miles southeast of Thyatira on the northern slopes of Mount Tmolus, *Sardis* dominates the Hermes River valley. In the sixth century B.C. under the "golden" Croesus, Sardis was capital of the Lydian kingdom. It was one of the great trading centers of the ancient world. Sardis was noted for its wool and dying industry.

The people of Sardis worshiped the Lydian Zeus. As polytheists they practiced the orgiastic cult of Cybele, the nature goddess. Emperor worship was practiced here, too. In gratitude to its benefactor, Tiberius, who enabled the city to rebuild after the earthquake, Sardis erected a temple in honor of Tiberius and Livia. Archaeological remains suggest that there was a synagogue here and a large colony of Jews.

Philadelphia lay about twenty-eight miles east of Sardis on the great way to the east. It stood where three countries met: Lydia, Phrygia, and Mysia. Founded for the purpose of spreading Greek culture in the highlands of the surrounding countryside, Philadelphia became known as "little Athens." It was also a wine center. The chief deity of the town was Dionysius, god of the vine and of drama. After the earthquake of 17 A.D. Philadelphia was rebuilt with the help of Emperor Tiberius and was involved in emperor worship.

Laodicea was a rich, proud, imposing city in the fertile Lycus valley. It lay on the southern side of the Lycus River some fifty-five miles southeast of Philadelphia and about ten miles west of Colosse. It was a great commercial and banking center and the seat of a famous medical school. Well-known products of Laodicea included eye salve as well as clothing and carpets manufactured from native black wool. Victim of the earthquake of 60 A.D. the proud city refused imperial aid and paid for rebuilding out of her own coffers. Worship of the emperor was introduced into Laodicea at an early date.

2. The Identification of the Speaker

The authority and solemnity of the messages to the churches would be felt by the worshiper as he stood and heard the first words of each letter, "Thus says (the Lord)." This formula used by the Old Testament prophets would go far to authenticate the message.

For the listening congregations the identity of the speaker would not be in doubt. All seven characterizations point to the Son of Man of chapter 1.

Nor would there be any doubt about the meaning of the symbols.
For the hearers these would be familiar phrases used in their theology
and worship for confessing faith in their sovereign Lord Jesus Christ.

He is the One who **walks** among the churches to comfort and confront.

He is the One who **was dead and is alive.**

He is the One whose discerning Word sharply discriminates between truth and falsehood.

He is the One who is **the Son of God, who has eyes like a flame of
fire and feet like burnished bronze.**

He is the One who has **the seven spirits of God and the seven stars.**

He is the One who has **the key of David,** the key to the kingdom,
**who opens and no one can shut and shuts and no one can
open.**

He is **the Amen, the faithful and true martyr, the beginning of
God's creation.**

Many of the designations have a particular relevance for the
church addressed. For example, in Pergamum, the capital of the
province, the sword of Christ's Word confronts the sword of Rome. In
Thyatira the Son of God whose eyes flame with fire and whose feet are
burnished brass challenges the sun god, Apollo Tyrimnaios, Son of
Zeus, and the pagan metal workers' guilds. For Philadelphia, the town
founded as an open door for spreading Greek culture, the true key to
the true kingdom is held by Christ who has the ultimate power to open
and to shut.

3. The Speaker's Knowledge

The sevenfold repetition of the words "I know" underscores Christ's
thoroughgoing knowledge of his churches. He is omniscient. As God
knows all so now the risen Christ knows all. He knows his people more
profoundly than they know themselves.

He knows the good works, the patient endurance, the opposition to
evil men and to heretics of Ephesus.

He knows the persecution, poverty, and slander that Smyrna
endures.

He knows that Pergamum did not deny the faith in the face of the
martyrdom of Antipas.

He knows that Thyatira is growing in good works, love, faith,
service, and patient endurance.

He knows the few spotless in Sardis.

He knows that Philadelphia has kept his word and not denied him. He knows that there is nothing good to say about Laodicea.

4. The Speaker's Criticisms

The risen Lord knows not only their virtues but also their faults. His keen discerning Word cuts through their pretenses and self-deceptions. Only Smyrna and Philadelphia are without fault. On all the others his sword falls.

The fire is gone from Ephesus' love.

The churches at Pergamum and Thyatira tolerate members who hold to false teachings and compromise with the local culture. Participating in feasts in idol temples and committing immorality are probably the sins involved. Christians who were members of metals workers' guilds in Thyatira would be subject to intense social pressure to participate in emperor worship and pagan feasts.

The church at Sardis had a good reputation but was spiritually dead. Aside from a few faithful and "spotless," the rest were nominal Christians who had made tragic compromises with their pagan environment.

Philadelphia has remained faithful and not denied Christ by word or deed but has little influence.

Rich, opulent Laodicea has been lulled by luxury into lukewarmness.

The speaker's and the prophet's understanding of the realistic situation confronting each of the seven congregations was far more profound than that conveyed by the simple listing of commendations and criticisms.

John knew what it was to live under the shadow of the Roman Empire. Rome was a benevolent tyrant. She demanded absolute loyalty from her subjects. At the same time she was very tolerant of native religions and customs. The official religion was that of the goddess Roma and the emperor. Each of the seven cities had its state shrine. Political loyalty involved participation in the feasts and festivals of the state cult.

Ephesus, for example, as depicted by Ethelbert Stauffer,[1] celebrated Domitian's assumption of imperial power with pomp and circumstance worthy of the Fourth of July. Domitian's image, four times life size, arrived at the harbor and was met by huge crowds. The imperial procession bearing the image moved towards the city. Another large procession with priestly and civic dignitaries came out from the city gate to meet it. Together in a mass procession with torches and hymns they escorted the image of the emperor and enthroned it in the new imperial temple amid candelabra, altars, and statues. The head of the cult of the emperor was also the high priest of Asia and the president of the government of the province now meeting in the new temple of Domitian.

5. The Commands to Individual Congregations

The admonitions of the Glorified Christ to the members of the seven churches assembled in worship are not suggestions. They are straightforward and clear. There is no mistaking their meaning. They ring with authority.

> Remember from what you have fallen! Repent! Do the works you did at first!
> Don't fear what you are about to suffer! Be faithful unto death!
> Change your life style!
> Hold fast to what you have!
> Awake! Strengthen what is left! Remember what you received! Keep that! Repent!

Only in the case of Laodicea are the words of admonition unique. They are specifically related to the proud opulence of the famed city. In place of the counterfeit cultural values of the Laodiceans the congregation is counseled to buy from Christ pure gold, **white garments** of purity to cover their wretchedness, and divine **salve** to anoint their eyes that they may see. Become zealous rather than lukewarm! "Repent!"

6. The Command to All

While the individual commands are specifically related to particular situations prevalent in the individual congregations they all have the same purpose. That purpose is to motivate members to Christian faith and action. It is Christ's intention that all remember the Christian teaching they received, that all repent if they have become lukewarm or fallen into immorality or departed from the faith, that all hold fast and strengthen what remains, that all remain faithful unto death. Every worshiper hearing the commands to the churches is himself to give heed and obey.

7. The Promises

Apart from the overall setting of the letters and the promises, a reader might suppose that the admonitions are such that any preacher might give to a worshiping congregation.

However, the language of the promises is the language of conflict, of crisis, of eschatology, i.e., of the end, the consummation of all things. The terms used are **conqueror** (or victor), **fruit from the tree of life in the paradise of God, the crown of life, protection from the second death, a white stone, a secret name, sitting on Christ's throne, power over the nations, the book of life, a pillar** in the heavenly temple. Only as a foretaste can they be understood to be the possession of faithful members of the seven churches now. They will be bestowed in the end-time of those who hold fast to the end, even if need be unto martyrdom. Only those who keep the commands of the resurrected Christ will receive the promised rewards.

Verse 20 of chapter 3 merits special comment. The context could be interpreted to indicate that the coming of Christ here is primarily eschatological. The coming referred to would be in the end-time and the meal would be the Messianic banquet (cf. Mark 13:29; Luke 12:36). However, the promises in Revelation may be entered into in an anticipatory "first fruits" way by the faithful even in this life. Certainly John was appealing to the Laodiceans and by implication to all wayward members of the seven churches to repent and open the door of the heart to Christ *now*. The individual character of the invitation, "if anyone . . . ," reinforces this interpretation. Charles aptly writes that Christ comes as a friend and seeks entrance to the individual's heart.[2]

Text: The Message to Ephesus 2:1-7
To the angel of the church in Ephesus write: 2:1
"This is the Word from the One who holds the seven stars
in his right hand, who walks in the midst of the seven
golden lampstands."

I know your works, both your labor and your steadfast en-   2
durance, that you cannot stand evil persons and that
you have tested those who call themselves apostles
and are not and found them to be liars.

You have endured with steadfastness and borne bur-   3
dens for my name's sake and not grown weary.

But I have this against you: 4
You have forsaken the love you had at first.

So remember the heights from which you have fallen and   5
repent and do the deeds you did at first.

If you don't repent, I will come to you and remove your
lampstand from its place.

But you have this in your favor, you hate the works of the   6
Nicolaitans which I also hate.

> *You who have ears to hear, hear what the Spirit says to*   7
> *the churches.*
> *I will grant to everyone who conquers the right to eat*
> *from the tree of life which is in the paradise of God.*

The Message to Smyrna 2:8-11
To the angel of the church in Smyrna write: 2:8
> *"This is the Word from the One who is the First and the*
> *Last, who was dead and now is alive."*
> *I know your tribulation and your poverty, but you are rich.*   9
> *I know the blasphemy of those who call themselves Jews,*
> *but are not. They are a synagogue of Satan.*
> *Don't fear what you are about to suffer.*   10
> > *Look, the devil is going to cast some of you into*
> > *prison to test you. You shall have tribulation for ten*
> > *days.*
> *Be faithful unto death and I will give you the crown of life.*
> *You who have ears to hear, hear what the Spirit says to*   11
> *the churches.*
> *The victor will not be hurt by the second death.*

The Message to Pergamum 2:12-17
To the angel of the church in Pergamum write: 2:12
> *"This is the Word from the One who has the sharp two-*
> *edged sword."*
> *I know that you live where Satan sits enthroned and that*   13
> *you are holding on to my name and did not deny your*
> *faith in me even in the days when Antipas stood by his*
> *testimony to me and was martyred right where Satan*
> *dwells.*
> *But I have a few things against you:*   14
> > *You have there some who hold to the teaching of*
> > *Balaam, who taught Balak to place a stumbling block*
> > *before the children of Israel enticing them to eat meat*
> > *sacrificed to idols and to commit fornication.*
> *You also have some who practice the teaching of the*   15
> *Nicolaitans.*
> *Now mend your ways! If you don't I shall come quickly*   16
> *and war against you with the sword that comes out of*
> *my mouth.*
> *You who have ears to hear, hear what the Spirit says to*   17
> *the churches.*
> *To the one who conquers, I will give hidden manna and a*
> *white stone on which is inscribed a new name which*

no one knows except the person who receives it.

The Message to Thyatira 2:18-29
To the angel of the church in Thyatira write: 2:18
"This is the Word from the son of God, who has blazing eyes and whose feet are like polished brass."
I know your works: your love and faith 19
your service and patient endurance and that you are accomplishing more than you did at first.
But I hold this against you: 20
you tolerate that woman, Jezebel, who calls herself a prophetess, who by her teaching deceives my slaves and entices them into committing fornication and eating food that has been sacrificed to idols.
I gave her time to repent of her immorality, but she would 21
not.
Therefore I shall strike her and her paramours down and 22
throw them into the same sick bed where they shall suffer untold agonies unless they change their ways.
And I will strike her children dead and all the church- 23
es will know that I am the One who searches minds and hearts. And I will give each of you what you deserve.
To the rest of you in Thyatira who do not hold to this 24
teaching, who have not learned what they call the deep secrets of Satan, I am not going to lay upon you any other burden.
Just hold firmly to what you have until I come. 25
To those who conquer, who continue to keep my com- 26
mands until the end, I will give power over the na-
tions. They shall rule them with an iron rod and break 27
them in pieces as clay pots. This is the same author-
ity I received from my Father.
I will give them the morning star as well. 28
You who have ears to hear, hear what the Spirit says to 29
the churches.

The Message to Sardis 3:1-6
To the angel of the church in Sardis write: 3:1
"This is the Word from the One who holds the seven spir-its of God and the seven stars."
I know what you are doing. You have the name of being alive but you are dead.

Wake up! Strengthen what remains for it is at death's   2
       door! I have not found a single thing you have carried
       to completion for God.

So remember how you eagerly accepted what you were   3
       taught. Repent and do it! Now if you don't wake up, I
       will come as a thief and you won't know the hour
       when I shall descend upon you.

But you still have a few persons in Sardis who have kept   4
       their garments clean. They shall parade with me in
       white robes for they are worthy.

The conquerors shall be robed in white garments and   5
       their names shall remain in the Book of Life. And I
       shall claim them as my own before my Father and his
       angels.

You who have ears to hear, hear what the Spirit says to   6
       the churches.

The Message to Philadelphia 3:7-13
To the angel of the church in Philadelphia write: 3:7
       "This is the Word of the Holy One and True, who possesses
       David's key,
              who opens and no one can shut,
              and shuts and no one can open."

I know what you are doing. I have given you a door—wide   8
       open—which no one can shut. You have a little
       power. Yet you have held to my message and not
       denied my name.

Now listen to this! Those of the synagogue of Satan, who   9
       call themselves Jews but are liars, I will make come
       and fall down at your feet and learn that I love you.

Because you have patiently held fast to God's saving pur-   10
       pose I will keep you from the hour of trial which is
       coming over the whole world to test the earth-
       dwellers.

I am coming soon! Hold fast to your crown! Let no one   11
       take it from you.

I will make the conquerors pillars in the temple of my God   12
       and they shall never leave it. And I shall inscribe on
       them the name of my God and the name of the city of
       my God, the new Jerusalem which comes down out
       of heaven from my God. And I shall write on them my
       own new name.

You who have ears to hear, hear what the Spirit says to   13
       the churches.

The Message to Laodicea 3:14-22

To the angel of the church in Laodicea write: 3:14

    "This is the Word of the Amen, the True and Faithful
      Martyr, the Beginning of God's Creation."

    I know your condition: you are neither hot nor cold. Would   15
      that you were cold or hot. So, since you are lukewarm,   16
      neither hot nor cold, I am going to spit you out
      of my mouth.

    You say, "I am rich and well off. I need nothing."   17
      You don't know that you are in fact wretched,
      pitiable, poor, blind and naked.

    I warn you therefore, buy from me refined gold that you   18
      may be rich, white clothes to put on to cover your
      nakedness, and salve to anoint your eyes so that you
      can see. Those whom I love I reprove and discipline.   19
      So be zealous and repent!

    Look! I am standing at the door knocking. If any one of   20
      you hears me calling and opens the door, I shall
      come in and stay with you as your guest and we shall
      tarry over dinner together.

    Those who conquer shall reign with me on my throne as I   21
      have conquered and reign with my Father on his
      throne.

    You who have ears to hear, hear what the Spirit says to   22
      the churches.

The Message

Though the letters were addressed to congregations in Asia Minor at the end of the first century A.D. their message is for Christians of every age. The temptations and situations are universal: initial love and zeal which tends to cool and become lukewarm in time; false teachers, Jezebels and Balaams who lead astray the immature and unwary; poverty, persecution, and slander; pretense and self-deception; compromise with a pagan culture and immorality; the deadly effect of riches and "self-sufficient" pride. These temptations confront Christians of every age.

The promises, too, are valid for all time. They form the content of Christian hope: victory over temptation and satanic adversaries, the crown of Life, participating in Christ's rule, fellowship with him in the presence of God, belonging to God's own people. The promises are variously stated in symbolic terms but they all mean the same thing: *Be faithful unto death and I will give you the crown of life* (2:10). The trials

44

and limitations of this life will be over; the faithful Christians will participate with Christ in his victory. They will reign and fellowship with him in the Kingdom of God. **He shall reign forever and ever!**

The invitation in 3:20 may be applied as a universal promise intended not only for those assembled in worship in the seven churches of Asia but for everyone who hears and accepts Christ's invitation. **Behold, I stand at the door and knock; if anyone hears my voice and opens the door, I will come in and eat with him and he with me.** Even now, in the midst of temptation, hardship, and tribulation the person who opens the door to Christ can have fellowship with him. Communion almost inevitably comes to mind. The Lord's supper is a foretaste of the intimate fellowship with Christ that will take place at the Messianic banquet to be celebrated in the Kingdom of God in the end-time.

---

1. Stauffer, E., *Christ and the Caesars*. Tr. K. and R. Gregor Smith. London: S.C.M. Press, 1955, chapter 11.
2. Charles, R. H., *A Critical and Exegetical Commentary on the Revelation of St. John* (The International Critical Commentary), 2 vols. Edinburgh: T & T Clark, 1920, in loc.

4
To God and to the Lamb
4:1—6:17

Introduction

Ideally 4:1 — 8:1 should be studied as a whole and experienced as a unit. The throne visions of 4 and 5 dominate the entire series. Because of the length of the sequence, 4 and 5 will be handled separately.

While the *focus* in the first vision was on the Glorified Christ, the *locus* (setting) was on earth among the seven churches of Asia. In chapters 4 and 5 the *locus* is in heaven. The *focus* is on God the Creator and Ruler who sits enthroned and on the Lamb, the Redeemer.

Here we have a new beginning. Here is the place the revelation of **what must take place after this** starts (4:1; cf. 1:1). Visions such as those of the seven seals, the seven trumpets, and the seven bowls follow one another in ever increasing intensity until they reach their climax in the battle of Armageddon, the last judgment, and the New Heaven and the New Earth.

The whole sequence begins in the worship scenes of 4 and 5 in the throne room in Heaven. By the end of the fifth chapter **every creature in heaven and on earth and under the earth and in the sea** joins in singing praises **to him who sits on the throne and to the Lamb.** This is a foundational vision not only for the opening of the seven seals which follows in 6:1 — 8:1, but also for the entire book of Revelation.

THE VISION OF GOD   4:1-11

The Vision
YOU ARE THERE!

Look!	In heaven an open door!	4:1
Listen!	The trumpet-voice John heard at first calls, *Come up here. I will show you what has to happen.*	
See!	John, filled with the Spirit, sees a	2

	throne in heaven!	
	Sitting on it One whose appearance resembles jasper and carnelian.	3
	Round the throne a rainbow brilliant as an emerald.	4
	Surronding the throne twenty-four thrones and on them twenty-four elders dressed in white with golden crowns.	
Look! Listen!	From the throne come lightning flashes, peals of thunder, and voices.	5
Look!	In front of the throne seven torches burning, a sea of glass, crystal clear.	6
	Round the throne four living creatures, full of eyes in front and back.	
	the first resembles a lion,	7
	the second resembles an ox,	
	the third has a face of a man,	
	the fourth resembles a flying eagle.	
	Each has six wings, filled with eyes on all sides and within.	8
Listen!	Day and night they sing unceasingly *Holy, Holy, Holy, is the Lord God Almighty who was and is and is to come!*	
Look!	Whenever the living creatures give honor and glory and thanks to Him who is sitting on the throne, who is alive forever more,	9
	the twenty-four elders cast their crowns and fall down and worship.	10
Listen!	They are singing, *You are worthy, our Lord and God, to receive glory and honor and power because you created all things and willed them to exist as your creation.*	11

Interpretation: What does the text say?

The mediator of this vision is the Glorified Christ of chapter 1. This is made clear by identifying the "voice" of 4:1 with "the first voice, which I had heard speaking to me like a trumpet." See 1:10, 12. This emphasizes the inseparability of the work of Christ from the saving purpose of God.

The meaning of the text is stated clearly in the two hymns (vv. 8 and 11). God is Lord! He is sovereign ruler. He is almighty. He is thrice holy. He is eternal. He was, he lives, he is coming. He is the creator of all. He is worthy of worship, of receiving glory and honor and power.

The meaning is enhanced and filled out by the artistry of the vision. Beauty and magnificence are depicted by precious stones, a rainbow, golden crowns, thrones, and white robes. Power, insight, omniscience are suggested by the seven torches, the seven Spirits of God, the flashes of lightning, peals of thunder, and four living creatures full of eyes.

The setting is the throne room in heaven. In addition to God's throne there are twenty-four other thrones and crowns. This symbolism suggests that under God's sovereignty the elders rule with him. They may represent the people of God of Israel and the Church.

The promise to the seven churches was that the faithful Christian would sit with Christ on his throne (3:21). In chapter 20, verse 4 the faithful martyrs reign with Christ for one thousand years. What even now is a reality in heaven (chapter 4) is to become a reality on earth (20:4).

THE VISION OF THE LAMB 5:1-14

Introduction

Chapter 5 is both a continuation of the vision of chapter 4 and a contrast to it. The scene still takes place in the throne room in heaven. God is still on the throne, but the action now centers around the Lamb and the scroll. The theme shifts from the sovereignty of God to the sovereignty of the Lamb and his life story. He is the one who was slain and by his blood ransomed men and women to God. The scene which was confined to the throne room in heaven and to the twenty-four elders and the four living creatures now encompasses the far reaches of the universe—to "every creature" in heaven, on earth, and under the earth.

Envision the stage as being the universe. A seven-sealed scroll is in the right hand of God. No one in the universe can be found worthy to open it. So John weeps. Then one of the elders tells John that the Lion of Judah, the Root of David can open it. John sees a

Lamb standing as though it has been slain. The Lamb comes and takes
the scroll. Then the four living creatures, the elders, myriads of angels,
and every living creature throughout the universe join in worshiping the
Lamb.

Vision 5:1-14

Let your imagination expand to include the throne room of God,
all of heaven, earth, and under the earth.

YOU ARE THERE!

See!	In the right hand of God who is seated on the throne is a scroll written within and on the back, sealed with seven seals.	5:1
Listen!	A Mighty Angel calls with a loud voice, *Who is worthy to break the seals and open the scroll?*	2
Look!	No one in heaven or on earth or under the earth is found fit to open the scroll and break its seals.	3
Look!	John begins to weep profusely and cry aloud because no one can be found qualified to open the scroll and see what is inside.	4
Listen!	Then one of the elders says, *John, stop crying! The Lion of the tribe of Judah, the descendant of David, is Victor. He has won the right to break the seven seals and to open the scroll.*	5
Look!	Standing in the midst of those around the throne, the four living creatures and the elders, there is a Lamb. The Lamb looks as if it has been sacrificed. It has seven horns and seven eyes.	6
Look!	The Lamb goes and takes the scroll from the right hand of him who sits on the throne.	7
Look!	The four living creatures and the twenty-four elders immediately prostrate themselves before the Lamb. Each holds a harp and golden bowl full of incense.	8

Listen!   They are singing a new song,   9
                You have earned the right to take
                the scroll and break its seals, for
                you were martyred. By your blood
                you have ransomed people for God
                from every tribe, tongue, people,
                and nation and made them a king-   10
                dom of priests for God. They are to
                rule over the earth.

Look!   Innumerable angels, ten thousand times   11
                ten thousand and thousands of
                thousands surround the throne.

Listen!   They are singing in a mighty chorus that   12
                can be heard in the farthest corner
                of the universe. *Worthy is the*
                Lamb who was slaughtered to
                receive power and wealth and wis-
                dom and might, and honor and
                glory and praise!

Look!   Every created being in heaven and on   13
                earth and under the earth and in
                the sea is singing!

Listen!   *To him who sits on the throne and to*
                the Lamb be praise and honor and
                glory and power for ever and ever!

Listen! Look!   *Amen!* shout the four living creatures   14
                and the twenty-four elders bow
                down in worship.

Interpretation: What does the text say?

The key to the interpretation is clearly stated by the writer in the hymns of verses 9-10, 12, and 13. The underlying theme of the first hymn is "God's Saving Purpose," namely, that his kingdom will come on earth as it is even now in heaven. His saving purpose is embodied and accomplished in the Lamb. By his death we have been redeemed. He has made us a kingdom of priests to God. By taking the scroll and opening its seals he is setting in motion the events of the end-time. The final outcome will be the coming of God's kingdom on earth in which his people shall reign. This is the message of the "new" song. It is "new" because the time is at hand.

Note that the initiative in opening the scroll is not taken by God. It cannot be taken by humans. Neither man nor woman has the power and wisdom and honor and glory necessary for the task. But the Lamb is worthy. He shares with God the power and wealth and wisdom and might and honor and glory and blessing. For he lived and died on earth and redeemed men and women to God.

The scroll is in God's hand. Presumably the message written on it is his will. The implication is that by opening the scroll God's saving purpose will come to pass.

God's saving purpose began in the act of creation and is completed in the redemption of persons from every **tribe, tongue and nation.**

The Message of Chapters Four and Five

The vision of God and of Christ set John the prisoner free. The exile was free! Freedom is not a matter of banishment or bonds or bounty. Freedom is a condition of the soul. It is available to everyone who shifts the focus of his or her life from earth to heaven, from self to God and the Lamb, from time to eternity.

Fundamental to a living faith for John, the members of the seven churches, and Christians of every age is faith in the sovereignty of God as Creator, Sustainer, and Ruler of the universe. Behind all the vicissitudes of history stands the Almighty. God is on the throne of the universe now. The hopes of humanity are dependent upon the enthronement of God.

By his death Christ has won the right to be worshiped as God is worshiped. He did for persons what they could not do for themselves. He did for humankind only what God could do. By his death he has redeemed persons to God from every tribe, tongue, people, and nation.

The hopes of the saints as expressed in their prayers are fulfilled by Christ's redemptive action. He made them a kingdom and gave them direct access as priests to God. Through the Lamb the prayer for the coming of God's kingdom on earth is certain of realization.

Worship is central to the plan of God in its beginning in creation and its fulfillment in the establishment of his kingdom on earth. In the context of worship, God's presence and his will become known. Worship engenders praise in the heart. In the coming kingdom the earth shall be filled with the worship of God as the waters cover the sea.

THE OPENING OF THE FIRST SIX SEALS   6:1-17

Introduction

The action which is about to begin in chapter 6 is closely knit to the throne visions of chapters 4 and 5 by the presence of the Lamb, the four Living Creatures, and the scroll with seven seals.

The seven seals comprise the first of three series of judgments (seven seals, seven trumpets, seven bowls) and the beginning of the revelation of **what must take place after this** (4:1, cf. 1:1). Each succeeding series intensifies the judgments. Finally with the seventh bowl of God's wrath, the great Voice from the throne in the heavenly temple proclaims "It is done!" (16:17)

The seals are divided into units of four, two, and one. An interlude (ch. 7) separates the first six from the seventh. The so-called "four horsemen of the Apocalypse," conquest, war, near famine, and death, are followed in the fifth seal by the cry from the martyrs under the altar, "How long, O Lord?" and the answer, "Rest a little longer." With the sixth seal comes the great judgment day of the wrath of God and the Lamb. The end has come! The seventh seal functions as an introduction to the trumpet series.

The action is directed from heaven. The Lamb in the presence of the throne is in charge. In directing the first four seals, the Four Living Creatures function as his agents.

The Vision of the First Six Seals   6:1-17

From your vantage place in God's royal court in heaven, watch the action taking place throughout the world.

YOU ARE THERE

Look!	The Lamb breaks open the first seal.	6:1
Listen!	The Lion roars, *Come!*	
Look!	A white horse and a rider! He's given a bow and a crown and rides forth victorious, conquering,	2
Look!	The Lamb breaks the second seal.	3
Listen!	The Ox bellows, *Come!*	
See!	Out comes a bright red war horse and a rider! He is given a huge sword; peace vanishes from the earth; men slay one another.	4
Look!	The Lamb breaks the third seal.	5
Listen!	The human-faced creature cries, *Come!*	
Look!	A black horse! Its rider holds a pair of scales in his hand.	
Listen!	From the midst of the four living creatures a cry,	6

*A day's wages for a quart of
wheat or three quarts of barley! But don't harm the oil or
wine!*

Look!	The Lamb breaks the fourth seal.	7
Listen!	The eagle poised to fly cries, *Come!*	
See!	A sickly-green horse! Death is its rider. Hades follows.	8

To them is given power over a quarter
of the earth to kill with the sword,
with famine, with pestilence, and
with wild beasts.

Look! The Lamb opens the fifth seal.   9

Look! Under the altar the souls of martyrs,
slaughtered for the Word of God
and the witness they had borne.

Listen! They cry aloud to high heaven,   10
*O Sovereign Master, holy and true,
how long before you will avenge
our blood and condemn those who
dwell on the earth?*

Look! To each is given a white robe and the   11
reassuring word:

Listen! *Rest a little while longer until the total
number of your fellow slaves and
brothers is complete, for they shall
be slaughtered as were you.*

Look! The Lamb breaks the sixth seal.   12

See! An earthquake, eight-point six on the
Richter scale!
The sun turns black as funeral
clothes.
The moon, blood-red.
The stars fall to the earth as   13
figs when a fig tree is shaken
by a gale.
The sky vanishes like a scroll   14
rolled up in a twinkling.
Every mountain and island
is shaken from its foundations.

Look! The kings of the earth, the great: the   15
generals, the rich, and the strong.

Listen!   Everyone cries out to the mountains   16
                     and rocks,
                          Fall on us!
                          Hide us from the awful pres-
                          ence of the Enthroned and
                          from the terrible wrath of the
                          Lamb!
                          The great day of their wrath is   17
                          here.
                          Who can stand before it?

Interpretation: What does the text say?

The key to the seal sequence lies in the fifth seal. **The souls of those who had been slain for the word of God and for the witness they had borne** are the martyrs who have died and now are **under the altar.** They shout, "How long will it be until you will judge the people of earth and punish them for killing us? Like the martyr Antipas of Pergamum (2:13), John, and other members of the seven churches, they have suffered at the hands of their persecutors. They cry out for justice. Their persecutors are the earth-dwellers who would be included among those mentioned in the sixth seal (v. 15), chiefly **the kings of the earth, the rulers and the military chiefs, the rich and the mighty.**

The answer to the insistent question of the martyrs, **How long. . . ?** is threefold: 1. **a little while longer** (v. 11); 2. **until the total number** of fellow Christians who were to be martyred was reached (v. 11); 3. **the great day of** the **wrath** of the Lamb and of God is at hand (vv. 16-17), i.e., the end-time is very close.

Prior to the end-time come the four horsemen of the first four seals. How are they to be interpreted? It is clear from the context that all that happens is under the sovereignty of God and in some sense is a consequence of the victory of the Lamb. By his death he has conquered (5:5, 9). The very dastardly deed of the forces of evil has been transformed by God into victory. It is as victor that the Lamb opens the seals. The Lamb in heaven is in ultimate control of what happens on earth.

The meaning of the first seal is disputed. Obviously it is a symbol of conquest. This white horse is similar to the horse in Revelation 19:11f. There the Word of God rides forth on a white horse in conquest to smite and rule the nations. This similarity has led some to interpret the first seal as representing the conquest of the gospel. The triumph of the gospel goes on at the same time that the terrible plagues of the other seals wreak their havoc. Others insisting that the first seal must be in harmony with the other three interpret the first seal and second seal as symbolizing war.

The third symbolizes near famine conditions; the fourth, death.

The disasters represented in the seals are severe but not yet catastrophic. Wheat and barley are still available though priced at a *denarius* (a day's wages). Oil and wine are in good supply (v. 6). Death and the grave (Hades) are allowed to claim only one-fourth of the earth (v. 8). Judgment is partial.

The sixth seal pictures the end of the world. It is the judgment of God on the persecutors of the martyrs (vv. 16-17, cf. v. 10). It is the vindication of those who have been faithful unto death.

5

The Trumpets

7:1—9:21

THE PEOPLE OF GOD AND THE LAMB

Introduction

Chapter seven is an interlude in the midst of the descriptions of the judgments of God. At the same time it is integral to understanding the entire vision of 4:1 — 8:1. It deals with God's people and their reward. This is the counterpoint to the judgments in the seals.

There are two scenes: the first on earth, the second in heaven. On earth 144,000 slaves of God (see page 14f) are sealed on their foreheads while four angels at the four corners of the earth hold back the four winds. In heaven is a prevision of the final outcome, the celebration with "those who have come out of the great tribulation" before the throne of God. An innumerable company from every nation, tribe, people, and tongue stand before God and the Lamb. They are clothed in white robes, hold palm branches in their hands and praise God and the Lamb for salvation. They are joined in worship by all the angels and the four living creatures. The Lamb is in their midst as shepherd and guide. They serve God, who supplies their every need and wipes away every tear.

The Vision of the 144,000 on Earth   7:1-8
YOU ARE THERE!

See!	Four angels stand at the four corners of the earth.	7:1
	They hold in check the four winds of the earth, to prevent them from wreaking havoc on the earth or sea or even on one tree.	
Look!	Another angel ascends from the rising of the sun.	2

	He carries the branding iron of the living God, and shouts to the four angels empowered to hurt the earth and the sea,	
Listen!	*Do not hurt the earth or the sea or the trees, until we have branded the slaves of our God upon their foreheads!*	3
Listen!	The number of the branded!	4
	One hundred and forty-four thousand from every tribe of God's people: twelve thousand branded from the tribe of	5

Judah	Naphtali	Issachar
Reuben	Manasseh	Zebulun
Gad	Simeon	Joseph
Asher	Levi	Benjamin

The Vision of the Countless Multitude in Heaven   7:9-17
YOU ARE THERE!

Look!	The throne room in heaven!	7:9
	A tremendous multitude too great to count. From every nation, from all tribes and peoples and tongues, standing before God's throne and before the Lamb, wearing white robes, waving palm branches.	
Listen!	They are shouting at the top of their lungs,	10
	Salvation belongs to our God who sits on the throne and to the Lamb!	
Look!	All the angels standing around the throne and around the elders and around the four living creatures fall on their faces and worship God saying,	11
Listen!	*Amen! Blessing and glory and wisdom and thanksgiving and honor and authority and might be to our God for ever and ever! Amen!*	12
Listen!	One of the elders is asking John,	13
	Who are these people wearing white robes? *Where do they come from?*	

Listen!	He replies, *You're my interpreter, you know.*	
Note This!	Then the elder says,	14

> These are those who have come
> out of the great tribulation;
> they have washed their robes and
> made them white in the Lamb's
> blood.

> Therefore, they have been granted   15
> a place in God's presence and
> serve him day and night in his tem-
> ple.
> God who sits on the throne will
> shelter them with his presence.

> They shall never hunger nor thirst,   16
> nor suffer from the heat of the sun
> or be scorched by any fire.

> For the Lamb in the heart of the   17
> throne will be their shepherd and
> guide them to springs of living
> water.
> And God will wipe every tear from
> their eyes.

Interpretation: What does the text say?

Before the breaking of the seventh seal and the terrible judgments that follow in the seven trumpets comes the interlude which is chapter 7. The purpose of the interlude is made clear in verses 1-3. The four winds are chafing at the bit, ready to harm the earth, the sea, and the trees. Four angels are told to hold back the four winds until **the slaves of God** have been **sealed upon their foreheads.** God will keep his people secure even through the destruction that is coming. In 16:2, the first bowl of God's wrath is poured on those who bear the mark of the Monster. This suggests that those bearing the seal or mark of God will be spared from the outpouring of his wrathful punishment.

One hundred and forty-four thousand is a symbolic number made up of twelve thousand from each of the twelve tribes of Israel. Not all are to be saved, but only the true **slaves of God.** That this is not Israel according to the flesh is suggested by the fact that the list of tribes does not correspond to any of the lists in the Old Testament. Members of the seven churches would understand this to include the faithful among their number, those *who overcome* and especially to those who are **faithful unto death** (2:10). This would not necessarily exclude the Old Testament saints.

In the second scene (vv. 13-17) the great tribulation (v. 14) is over. An innumerable multitude from every nation stands before the throne in heaven and worships God and the Lamb. They are the saved, those who have been faithful and have come through the great tribulation (vv. 10, 14). **They have washed their robes and made them white in the blood of the Lamb** (v. 14). This suggests that they are martyrs or at least include the martyrs.

Their reward is pictured in verses 15-17. They serve God. All their needs are supplied; the Lamb will guide them to living water; God will wipe every tear from their eyes. This is a preview of the New Heaven and the New Earth of 21:1-4.

Message

The purpose of this vision is the reassurance of the faithful. Even though the earth may quake, the mountains be removed, and the sky vanish (6:12-17) God has not forsaken his people. He cares for them even through destruction and turmoil. It is faith not faithlessness that triumphs over trouble. The Christian's inner security cannot be destroyed by outward circumstance.

God is still on the throne. He is still in control of all the powers in the universe. They are still subject to his authority. De-throning God cannot solve the great problems of the world. It can only compound them.

With God the future is secure. Faith becomes hope and hope is in the process of being realized. This is not the popular philosophy of Pollyanna. Tragedy is real. The churches of Asia still face sorrow, suffering, and even martyrdom. But the person of faith can look forward with confidence to the white robe of victory and a place before the throne of God and the Lamb.

One further note, as the recipient of God's grace, his unmerited favor, the faithful Christian is spared the lash of God's wrath. God's judgment falls on the wicked and the unrepentant.

The Message of 4:1—8:1

The promise of the Glorified Christ to the church at Smyrna, "Be faithful unto death and I will give you the crown of life" (2:10) is not far from the central message of chapters 4:1—8:1. The vision began in heaven with the twenty-four elders and the four living creatures worshiping God the Creator and Ruler. In chapter 5 they are joined by the redeemed, innumerable angels and "every creature" in worshiping God and Christ the Redeemer who are *worthy* of worship.

The tribulations of the seals follow. They are so severe and persistent that those who have been martyred cry out for justice. Their vindication comes with the falling of the wrath of God on the *earth-dwellers*, their persecutors. These are the kings of the earth, the rulers and the military chiefs, the rich and the mighty, and their lesser followers.

The vision ends in heaven after the tribulation with the twenty-four elders, the four living creatures, and an innumerable multitude of the redeemed worshiping God and the Lamb in the fulfilled Kingdom. To them be **blessing and honor and glory and power for ever and ever, Amen.**

Revelation as well as the Westminster Catechism proclaims, "Our chief end is to glorify God and enjoy him forever." Worship of the Creator and Redeemer, with all that implies in terms of commitment and service, is at the heart of the meaning of life. The redeemed are **before the throne of God and serve him day and night within his temple (7:15). They shall never hunger . . . for the lamb . . . will be their shepherd . . . and God will wipe away every tear from their eyes.**

SOUNDING OF THE TRUMPETS   8:1—9:21

Introduction

The opening of the seventh seal introduces a second series of judgments, the seven trumpets. The third series, the seven bowls of God's wrath, will come later (cf. chap. 15f.). The content of the seventh seal consists of the judgments of the seven trumpets.

The grand sweep of events in the visions of the seven trumpets is similar to the movement of thought in chapters 4:1—8:1. Both sections begin in the throne room in heaven in a worship setting (4—5; 8:1-5). Both end in triumph, again in a worship setting (7:13-17; 11:15-19). God's decisive, powerful action is an answer to the prayers of the saints. In the seal sequence the saints under the altar cry out for justice (6:9-11). In the trumpet sequence the prayers of the saints rise up to God (8:3-4). He answers with the woes of the seven trumpets.

The contrast with the previous vision (ch. 7) could hardly be stronger. There in heaven the kingdom has come. Earthly trials are over. There harmony, peace, joy, and plenty are prevalent. Here on earth there is grievous travail and tribulation and woe heralded by the first six trumpets. In this section the reader must wait until the seventh trumpet to see that the Kingdom of God has come (11:15).

The setting for the blowing of the seven trumpets is the throne room in heaven. Seven angels standing before God are given seven trumpets. In response to the prayers of the saints the angel at the altar takes his incense burner, fills it with coals from off the altar, and throws it on earth. The thunder roars, lightning flashes, the earth quakes! Then the seven angels blow their trumpets in sequence and the judgments of God follow.

The trumpet sequence is as follows:
1. The first trumpet brings fire on one-third of the *earth*.
2. The second trumpet results in destruction of one-third of the *sea*.
3. The third trumpet poisons one-third of the *fresh waters*.
4. The fourth trumpet darkens one-third of the *heavens*.
5. The fifth trumpet brings a locust horde to torture the *wicked*.
6. The sixth trumpet brings two hundred million *demonic horsemen* from the river Euphrates.
(Interlude: 10:1—11:14)
7. The seventh trumpet heralds the coming of the *kingdom of God*.

Note that as in the case of the seals, so here between the sixth and seventh trumpets there is an interlude. In it John eats a little scroll (ch. 10) and two faithful witnesses are martyred and taken to heaven (11:1-14).

When the seventh trumpet sounds, the end has come. **The kingdom of the world has become the kingdom of our Lord and of his Christ . . . forever and ever** (11:15). Then the elders fall on their faces and worship God.

The Vision of the First Six Trumpets 8:1—9:21
You are with John in the throne room in heaven.
YOU ARE THERE!

Look!	The Lamb is opening the seventh seal.	8:1
Listen!	All heaven becomes silent for half an hour.	
Look!	Seven angels stand before God.	2
	They are given seven trumpets.	
Look!	Another angel swinging a golden censer approaches the altar.	3
	He is given a large amount of incense.	

He mingles it with the prayers of all the
  saints upon the golden altar.

Look!   Clouds of incense rise with the prayers   4
               of the saints to God.

Look!   Then the angel takes the censer in his   5
               hands,
                 fills it with burning coals from the
                 altar,
                 and hurls it down to earth.

Listen!   The thunder rolls, loud cries arise,
               tremendous flashes of lightning illumine
                 the entire sky,
               the earth quakes!

Look!   The seven angels raise their trumpets.   6
                 They are ready to blow.

Listen!   The first angel blows!   7
Look!   Hail, fire, mixed with blood falls on the
                 earth.
                 A third of the earth is consumed.
                 A third of the trees are burnt up.
                 And all the green grass turns into
                 ashes.

Listen!   The second angel blows his trumpet!   8
Look!   A huge burning mountain is hurled into
                 the sea.
                 A third of the sea turns to blood.   9
                 A third of the creatures that live in
                 the sea die.
                 A third of the ships burn up and
                 their passengers perish.

Listen!   The third angel blows!   10
Look!   A gigantic star blazing like a torch falls
                 from heaven.
                 A third of the springs and rivers   11
                 turn into wormwood.
                 Countless people drink the poi-
                 soned water and die.

Listen!   The fourth angel blows his trumpet!   12
Look!   The blast strikes a third of the sun, a
                 third of the moon, and a third of
                 the stars.
                 A third of their light burns out.
                 A third of the daylight fails.

	And a third of the night.	
Look!	A mighty eagle flies in mid-heaven shouting loud enough to be heard around the world.	13
Listen!	*Woe, woe, woe! to all peoples of the world for the three other angels are about to blow their blasts.*	
Listen!	The fifth angel blows his trumpet!	9:1
Look!	A star falls from heaven to earth.	
Look!	He is given the key to the door of the bottomless pit.	
Look!	Smoke as from a huge furnace billows from the pit and darkens the sun and the air.	2
Look!	Out of the smoke come swarms of locusts who possess the sting of scorpions in their tails.	3
Look!	The locusts look like horses equipped for battle: golden crowns adorn their heads; their faces are like human faces; their hair is like women's hair; their teeth like lion's teeth; they have iron breastplates; their wings clatter like chariots rushing into battle.	7 8 9
	Their king is the angel of the bottomless pit. His name in Hebrew is *Abbadon,* in Greek, *Apollyon,* in English, *Destruction.*	11
Listen!	A voice cries,	4
	Don't harm any living plant or tree! Sting only those people who do not bear God's brand on their foreheads.	
	Torture them for five months until they seek death and can't find it, and long to die but death flees from them.	5 6
Hark!	The first woe has passed. Be prepared! Two woes are yet to come!	12
Look!	The sixth angel lifts up his trumpet and blows.	13
Look!	From the four horns of the golden altar	

	that stands before God a voice commands the sixth angel,	14
Listen!	*Release the four angels who are bound at the great river Euphrates!*	
Look!	The four angels held ready for this very minute, hour, day, month, and year are set free to slaughter a third of humanity.	15
Look!	Two hundred million horsemen follow the four angels.	16
	The riders wear breastplates, fiery red, blue, and sulphur-yellow.	17
	The horses have lions' heads and tails like serpents with piercing fangs.	
Look!	The calvary charges forth belching fire, smoke, and sulphur. They slaughter one third of humanity.	18
Look!	The rest of humanity not killed by the plagues do not repent of their deeds: their murders, sorceries, fornication, and robberies, but continue worshiping demons and idols of gold and silver and bronze and stone and wood, which do not see, hear, or walk.	20 21

Interpretation: What does the text say?

Basic to understanding this vision and the entire book of Revelation is the realization that everything that happens is under the permissive, sovereign will of God and the action of the Lamb. **The Lamb** opens the seventh seal. The seven angels **stand before God.** The setting is the **throne** room in heaven at the **altar** (8:3-4). It is from the very presence of God that the seven trumpet blasts come. In the vision two hundred million horsemen, instruments of judgment, are set loose at the command from God's golden altar.

Does John think of **the saints** (v. 3) as being under the altar (as in 6:9)? If so they have already offered their lives as a sacrifice to God. Prayer is the only thing they have left to offer to him.

The judgments that follow are the response of God to their prayers —it is God's **altar** from which the **fire** of judgment is hurled (8:3-5). **The prayers of the saints** are important to God. Prayer as the cry of the heart may be the greatest gift one can offer to God. The content of the prayers of the saints is not specifically mentioned. However their petition may be inferred from 6:10 and 11:15. In the former the prayer is for the coming of the End and for justice. The actions initiated by the Lamb and by God's trumpeting angels may be understood as the intermediate answer. The ultimate answer is in verse 15 of chapter 11, **The kingdom of this world has become the kingdom of our Lord and of his Christ!**

The judgments of God involve the cooperation of natural phenomena. The **fire** is taken from the altar (God's altar) and hurled onto the earth. The **thunder** roars, the **lightning** flashes, the **earth** quakes (8:5).

The world of nature suffers along with humans from the plagues. **One-third of the earth** and **trees** and **all the green grass** are **burnt up. One-third of the sea** turns to **blood, one-third of** the marine life died. **One-third of the waters** become **wormwood** (8:7-11).

However, the point at issue is the judgment that falls on humans. Only six verses are given to judgments on nature while the entire ninth chapter is given over to the judgments on earth-dwellers. They do not have **the seal of God on their foreheads** (9:4). They are not protected from his wrath.

Yet the purpose of God's judgments is not basically punishment and retribution but **repentance** and salvation. It is his desire that men and women worship him, not demons and idols (9:20-21).

The judgments of God are tempered with mercy. The **locusts** were allowed only **five months** in which to **torture** people (9:5). The **two hundred million** horsemen were permitted to kill only **one-third** of humankind (9:15, 18).

At this point at the end of the sixth trumpet, God's saving purpose is thwarted by the earth-dwellers for they continue to worship the works of their hands, demons, and idols. **Nor** do they **repent of their murders or their sorceries or their immorality or their theft** (9:20-21).

6

Between Trumpets
10:1—11:19

THE LITTLE SCROLL   10:1-11

Introduction

Just as the seal series contained an interlude between the sixth and seventh seals, so here the trumpet series contains an interlude between the sixth and seventh trumpets (10:1—11:14). There the interlude functioned to reassure and comfort the seven churches facing persecution. The function of the present interlude will be considered later.

The vision in chapter 10 concerns a tremendous angel, a little scroll, and the prophet John. The vision in 11:1-14 tells about the measuring of the temple and the life story of the two witnesses. Then in 11:15-19 the blowing of the seventh trumpet heralds the coming of the kingdom of God.

A tremendous angel comes down from heaven holding a little scroll in his hand. When he speaks, seven thunders sound. But John is not allowed to write down what they say. The angel lifts up his right hand to heaven and swears, "There shall be no more delay!"

John goes up and takes the little scroll from the hand of the angel. The angel tells him to eat the scroll. John does so. It is sweet as honey in his mouth but bitter to his stomach. He is then told that he must prophesy further about many kings and tongues, and peoples, and nations.

Chapter 10 is another of those introductory passages which set the stage for what is coming. The scale is again gigantic. An angel of formidable proportions is wrapped in a cloud; he is as tall as a rainbow; his face is like the sun; his legs pillars of fire. How tall would the angel have to be? Don't picture him as on the beach with a wave lapping over one foot! **He set his right foot on the sea and his left foot on the land** . . . Land and sea are subject to him. His speech is so loud it sounds like the roaring of a lion, loud enough to awaken the seven thunders (10:3).

Vision 10:1-11
Free your imagination! Be guided by the text!
YOU ARE THERE!

Look!	A gigantic angel coming down from heaven! He is wrapped in a cloud; a rainbow crowns his head; his face is like the sun; his legs, pillars of fire.	10:1
	He has a little scroll unrolled in his hand.	2
Look!	He places his huge right foot on the sea, and his huge left foot on the land.	
Listen!	He is shouting with a voice that sounds like a lion roaring. Seven thunders thunder.	3
Look!	John takes up his pen and is about to write down what the seven thunders said, but . . .	4
Listen!	A voice from heaven commands, *Don't write down what the seven thunders have said! Seal it up!*	
Look!	The angel standing on sea and land lifts up his mighty arm to heaven and swears by the everliving God, Creator of heaven, earth, and sea, and all that is therein,	5 6
Listen!	*There shall be no more delay.* *When the time comes for the seventh angel to sound his trumpet, the hidden purposes of God which he announced to his slaves, the prophets, will be accomplished.*	7
Listen!	From heaven a voice commands John again, *Go, take the open scroll from the hand of the mighty angel who stands with one foot on the sea and one on the land.*	8
Look! Listen!	John goes up to the angel and says, *Give me the little scroll.*	9
Listen!	The angel replies, *Take it and eat; it will be bitter to your stomach, but sweet as honey in your mouth.*	
Look!	John takes the little scroll from the hand of the angel and eats it.	10
	It is sweet as honey in his mouth, but turns sour in his stomach.	
Listen!	The angel tells John,	11

*Again you must prophesy about many
peoples, nations, tongues, and kings.*

Interpretation: What does the text say?

This chapter is dominated by the **mighty angel coming down
out of heaven** and by the open **scroll** which he holds in his hand.
Since he comes from heaven and is mighty, what he has to say is from
God and is therefore certain and true. The fact that the scroll is open
means that its message is open to John. He eats it. It becomes a
part of him. The scene is reinforced by the **voice from heaven**. This is
either God's voice or someone with the authority to speak for God. The effect is to underscore the certainty and truth of what is said.

There are four key statements in this chapter:

1. *There shall be no more delay!*
2. *The mystery of God will be fulfilled.*
3. *It will turn sour in your stomach but be sweet as honey in your
   mouth.*
4. *You must prophesy about many peoples . . .*

The first two belong together. **The mystery of God announced to
his slaves the prophets**, that is, God's saving purpose is going to be
fulfilled when the **seventh angel** blows his **trumpet**.

The last two also belong together. John's commission to prophesy is
reinforced. What he has to say will be both sour and sweet. It will
contain both good news and bad news, salvation and judgment. In the
light of the first nine chapters we can infer that it will also mean suffering, persecution, and possible martyrdom for the faithful.

The **little scroll** inevitably calls to mind the larger **scroll sealed
with seven seals** of chapter 5. There Christ opened the seals revealing
the working out of God's saving purpose. Here the prophet John is the
channel of God's message. It is possible that John intends the content of
the little scroll to include chapters 12-22.

Message

For John. John is confirmed in his conviction that he has been com-
missioned by God as a prophet to make known to his people God's saving
purpose. He does not speak on his own authority but on the authority of
God. The authority of God is manifest in the **voice from heaven** and in
the **mighty angel** who as God's envoy has power over **land and sea**.

For the seven churches in Asia. The cry of the martyrs, "How
long . . . ?" is the cry of the members of the seven churches. The answer

at 6:11 was "just a little longer." Here the assurance is **"There shall be no more delay!"** This would bring shouts of joy to congregations facing heretics, poverty, persecution, and possible martyrdom. But sweetness would have its sour side as they realize the afflictions that they would probably suffer in the course of the realization of God's saving purpose.

Implications for many peoples and nations and tongues and kings. God's patience is on the verge of being exhausted. The time for repentance is almost over. Repent now or suffer the consequences.

THE TWO WITNESSES   11:1-19

Introduction

Revelation 11:1-14 forms the second half of the interlude between the sixth and seventh trumpets. It includes the measuring of the temple and the life stories of the two witnesses.

Revelation 11:15-19 forms the content of the seventh trumpet. It is another pre-vision of the end. Just as the sublime portrayal of the redeemed in heaven in 7:9-17 was followed by the plagues called forth by the six trumpet blasts, so the pre-vision of the coming of the Kingdom of God in chapter 11 is followed by the emergence of the dragon, the beast, the false prophet, and eventually by the seven bowls of wrath in chapters 12-16.

In 11:1-2 John measures the temple of God, the altar, and the worshipers but does not measure the court of the Gentiles.

Verses 3-14 tell the life story of God's two witnesses. For 1,266 days they have the power to prophesy and work miracles. When their witness is finished, they are killed by the monster from the bottomless pit. Their bodies lie on the street of the city where their Lord was crucified. After three and one-half days God resurrects them and they ascend to heaven in a cloud. A great earthquake follows. Seven thousand people are killed. The rest give glory to God.

The Visions   11:1-14
YOU ARE THERE!

Look!	John is given a long cane, a kind of meter stick, and is told,	11:1
Listen!	*Go and measure God's temple and altar and the worshipers, but do not measure the court outside the temple for it has been given over to the Gentiles. They will trample the Holy City underfoot for*	2

	forty-two months.	
	I will grant my two witnesses authority	3
	to prophesy for 1,266 days.	
Look!	The two witnesses are like two olive trees, like lamps that stand in the presence of God and never are out of his sight.	4
Look!	Fire is pouring forth from their mouths and devouring their enemies.	5
	They are shutting up the sky so no rain will fall while they are prophesying.	6
	They turn water into blood and smite the earth with plagues.	
Look!	They've finished their testimony.	7
Look!	The beast from the bottomless pit is warring against them.	
	He's conquering them. He's killing them!	
	Their bodies are lying in the street of the great city called "Sodom" and "Egypt," where their Lord was crucified.	8
Look!	For three and one-half days people from the tribes and tongues and languages and nations of the earth gaze upon their	9
	corpses and refuse them burial, re- joicing, celebrating and exchanging	10
	presents because the two prophets, thorns in the side of earth-dwellers, are now dead.	
Look!	After three and one-half days God breathes into them the breath of life.	11
	They stand on their feet.	
	Terror grips the crowds.	
Listen!	A loud voice from heaven calls, *Come up here!*	12
Look!	In the sight of their enemies they are taken up to heaven in a cloud.	
	The earth shakes violently.	13
	A tenth of the city falls and seven thou- sand are killed.	
	The rest are stricken with terror and give	

glory to the God of heaven and earth.

Listen!	*The second woe has passed; beware, the third woe is soon to come!*	14

The Vision of the Seventh Trumpet 11:15-19
YOU ARE THERE!

Look!	The seventh angel blows his trumpet.	11:15
Listen!	Loud voices in heaven shout,	
	The sovereignty of this world has passed over to our Lord and his Christ and he shall reign forever and forever!	
Look!	Then the Twenty-four Elders enthroned before God fall on their faces and worship,	16
Listen!	*We thank you, Lord God, the All-powerful. You are and always have been the All-powerful, but now you have taken up the reins of your full power, and begun to rule.*	17
	The Gentiles rage for your wrath has come. The time for the dead to be judged. The time for rewarding your slaves, the prophets, the saints those who worship you, both small and great. The time for destroying the destroyers of the earth.	18
Look!	The doors of the temple in heaven open. The ark becomes visible.	19
	Lightning flashes, thunder peals, the earth quakes, and a heavy hail falls.	

Interpretation: What does the text say?

Revelation 11:1-14 is perhaps the most difficult section in the book of Revelation to interpret. It is clear that most of the chapter must be interpreted symbolically. See, for example, verse 4, **These are the two olive trees** . . . In all probability the members of the seven churches would know the meaning of the symbols. However the author does not tell the reader explicitly what the meaning is. For this reason the interpreter must not be dogmatic in his conclusions. The most important issues are as follows:

1. The identity of **the great city** (v. 8). This is the one item in the chapter which John indicates is to be understood literally. **The great city** is the city **where their Lord was crucified,** i.e., Jerusalem. But the earthly Jerusalem for John is clearly a wicked city, not a holy city. So he calls it symbolically, **Sodom and Egypt.**

2. It follows that **the holy city** of verse 2 is not the earthly Jerusalem. It may symbolize the church where God and his people dwell. The fact that it will be trampled over may indicate the persecution John sees ahead for Christians.

3. The measuring of the Temple. John measures **the temple, the altar and those who worship there. Those who worship** presumably would be God's people, the New Israel. Apparently they are protected (measured) for a symbolic length of time, **forty-two months.** The outer court, i.e., the court of the Gentiles is **given over to the Gentiles.** They trample the city for **forty-two months.**

This may mean that God remembers his people even during persecution and brings the faithful through safely.

Alternately this may be a reflection of the protection, death, resurrection, and exaltation theme which is developed in more detail and clarity in the life story of the two witnesses (11:3-14).

4. The life story of the two witnesses (11:3-14). God's two witnesses prophesy and work miracles for **1,266 days**, equal to forty-two months. These two witnesses are prophets (v. 6) who speak God's message to the peoples.

Their life story is modeled on that of their Lord Jesus (v. 8, etc.). They are killed by their enemies. After three and one-half days they are resurrected and ascend to heaven in a cloud. A great **earthquake** destroys a tenth of the city. **Seven thousand people are killed. The rest give glory to God.**

The witnesses may represent Christian prophets like John. They speak for God until their work is accomplished. Then they suffer martyrdom at the hands of their enemies, are resurrected, and taken to heaven. God's judgment falls on their persecutors. Here giving **glory to God** may possibly be interpreted as repentance.

The life story of the witnesses may also be intended to be a model for the members of the seven churches of Asia. "Be faithful unto death and I will give you the crown of life" (2:10).

5. The Seventh Trumpet. The fulfillment of God's saving purpose is proclaimed as if it were already accomplished. **The kingdom of the world has become the kingdom of our Lord and of his Christ, and he shall reign for ever and ever.** However verses 17-18 indicate that the end is just now here. His **wrath** has come (v. 18). The time for judgment, for **rewarding** his **prophets** and people, and **for destroying the destroyers of the earth** has just come.

The setting for all that happens in chapters 4-11 is a worship service in the throne room in heaven. It is explicit here at the end of chapter 11 as it was at the beginning of chapter 4.

The divine response affirming the declarations of the hymn indicated that the end is at hand. The **temple in heaven is opened.** There is **lightning, thunder,** and **earthquake,** and **heavy hail.** These phenomena indicate that God is beginning to take action.

The Message of Chapters 4-11

Again and again this keynote is struck: God is in control of history. He is the sovereign ruler, not the kings of the earth, the generals, the rich and the strong (6:15). God will bring history to fulfillment in the kingdom of God and of his Messiah (11:15).

God does not forget his people. They are in his constant watch and care (11:1f, 7:1f, 6:10-11).

In daily life this does not mean joy without sorrow or victory without struggle. The way of Christ is the way of the Christian: through death to life, defeat to victory, tragedy to triumph (5:9-11, 7:14-17, 11:7-12).

The breath of God is the source of **life** (11:11).

The faithful will reap their reward. **They shall never hunger or thirst** or sorrow for **the Lamb will be their shepherd and guide them to springs of living water and God will wipe away every tear from their eyes** (7:16, 17).

The defeat of evil is the time of rejoicing for the good (11:17f).

The worship of God and the Lamb is the key to the meaning of life and death. In the beginning (chs. 4-5) the middle (7:9-17) and the end (11:15-19) of this section, John brings his readers into the very presence of God. They, too, with the innumerable company in heaven sing, **Worthy art thou, our Lord and God . . . Worthy is the Lamb that was slain . . . The kingdom of the world has become the kingdom of our Lord and of his Christ, and he shall reign for ever and ever** (4:11, 5:12, 11:15).

As for John and his fellow prophets, John's call to prophetic vocation is reaffirmed. God's message must become a part of him. It is both sweet and bitter. It tells of his care and redemption of his people as well as the travail they must endure and of God's judgment on evil. The prophet is to take as model the life of his Lord. Triumph and tragedy are a part of it; death and resurrection.

The prophet will be a member of that great company before God's throne who shout, **The Kingdom of the world has become the kingdom of our Lord and of his Christ, and he shall reign for ever and ever!**

7

War in Heaven and on Earth
12:1—13:18

Introduction

Chapters 1-11 mark the first "great cycle of visions."[1] With the resurrection of the two witnesses (11:11) and their ascension to heaven (11:12) the events of the end-time might be said to enter their last phase. Judgment falls (11:13), people repent (11:13b), and give glory to God (11:13c). Then with the blowing of the seventh trumpet the heavenly voices proclaim, "The kingdom of the world has become the kingdom of our Lord and of his Messiah. . . . " (11:15).

However the heavenly reality, the kingdom of God, has not yet become visible on earth. Perhaps for this reason, John makes a new start beginning with chapter 12.

The second cycle of visions begins with 12:1 and continues through 22:5. In the second cycle the great struggle between God and the devil ends much as it did in the first, with the establishment of the Kingdom of God. The political character of the struggle between the people of God and the earth-dwellers is more explicit in the second cycle. While still written in symbolic language, the material in chapters 12f weaves into the visions the political and religious historical conditions of the end of the first century A.D. Here, also, the picture of the Kingdom of God is more extensively filled out by the visions of the New Jerusalem and the New Eden.

Chapters 12-14 form an interlude between the woes of the seven trumpets and the terrible judgments of the seven bowls of the wrath of God. Here the momentous struggle between the forces of good and the forces of evil comes into gigantic, cineramic portrayal. God and his followers are locked in mortal combat with the devil and his cohorts, but there is no question as to the outcome.

Woven in brilliant colors in the tapestry of John's words, the spiritual struggle between good and evil is seen first in heaven and then on earth. There the two monsters, fully-empowered representatives of the Devil deceive the earth-dwellers and persecute the *saints*, i.e., the faithful Christians. But the Lamb and the faithful triumph. Judgment falls on the Vicious Monster and his followers.

In this sequence earth becomes a mirror of heaven. War in heaven, waged by the Devil against Michael and the angels, is reflected in war on earth. The monsters and their cohorts, the earth-dwellers, fight against the saints. The victory in heaven is mirrored in the victory of the Lamb celebrated on Mount Zion by the redeemed.

The visions of Revelation seem to outdo each other in grandeur and scope. That of chapter 12:1-6 is so gigantic that it encompasses the heavens. The vision of the Glorious Mother, so huge that she is clothed with the sun and has the moon under her feet and is crowned with twelve stars, staggers the imagination. Equally large is the Great Red Dragon with seven heads crowned with seven diadems and ten horns. With one sweep of his tail he accomplished the impossible feat of casting down one-third of the stars onto the earth. The Great Red Dragon stood before the Glorious Mother waiting to devour her offspring but her new-born son was caught up to the throne of God and the Glorious Mother fled away into the wilderness to a place God prepared for her.

In the second vision of this chapter we witness the tremendous battle in heaven between Michael and his angels and the Great Red Dragon with his angels. The Great Red Dragon and his angels, ignominiously defeated, are cast out of heaven and onto the earth.

There he takes out after the Glorious Mother who had borne the male child. With the gift of wings of an eagle she flies into the wilderness. Just as the flood pouring from the mouth of the Dragon is about to engulf her, the benevolent earth opens its mouth and swallows the river, and she is saved. The Great Red Dragon, frustrated and angry, goes off to make war on the rest of her offspring.

The Vision of the Glorious Mother and Her Child   12:1-6
YOU ARE THERE!

Look!   In heaven a great omen appears!   12:1
                      A Woman, the Glorious Mother
                      sheathed with the sun,
                      the moon beneath her feet,
                      crowned with twelve stars,
                      pregnant, at the very point   2

	of giving birth.	
Listen!	She cries out in birth pangs for delivery.	
Look!	In heaven another omen!	3
	A gigantic Red Dragon with seven heads and ten horns.	
	On his heads are seven crowns.	
	With one sweep of his tail	4
	he hurls one-third of the stars to earth.	
Look!	The Great Red Dragon stands before the pregnant Mother ready to devour the newborn infant.	
Look!	The Glorious Mother gives birth to a son, destined to rule the Gentiles with an iron rod.	5
Look!	Her son is snatched away to God and his throne.	
Look!	The Glorious Woman flees to the wilderness, to a place prepared for her by God,	6
	where she will be cared for for 1,260 days.	

The Vision of the Victory in Heaven   12:7-12
YOU ARE THERE!

Look!	Fighting in heaven! Michael and his angelic armies are fighting against the Great Red Dragon and his hosts.	12:7
Look!	Michael defeats the Great Red Dragon, the Ancient Snake, often called the Devil and Satan, the seducer of the whole world.	8
	He hurls him with his angels down to the earth.	9

Listen to the proclamation from heaven!

	Now the salvation and power and the kingdom of our God and the authority of his Messiah have come.	10
	The Devil, the Great Red Dragon, the prosecutor of our brethren	
	who accused them night and day in the court of heaven,	

has been thrown out of court
and cast down to earth.

Now hear this!

Our brethren have conquered him   11
by the blood of the Lamb of God
and by the witness of their lives.
They did not shrink from a martyr's
death for the love of life.

Listen!

Celebrate, O heaven, and all who dwell   12
therein!
But woe to you, O earth and sea,
for the Devil, the Great Red
Dragon, has come down to you.
He is furious for he knows his time
is short.

The Vision of the Dragon Chase on Earth   12:13-17
YOU ARE THERE!

Look!

The Great Red Dragon is on earth!   12:13
He is chasing the Glorious Mother.

Look!

She is given two enormous wings.   14
With them she flies away to her hide-
away in the wilderness where she
will be nourished for a time, times,
and a half a time.

Look!

The Great Red Dragon like a river at   15
flood time spews a tremendous
volume of water to sweep her away
to destruction.

See!

In the nick of time the earth opens its   16
mouth, swallows the river, and
saves the Glorious Mother.

See!

The Dragon, more furious than ever,   17
becomes scarlet with anger and
rushes off to war against the rest of
the Woman's children, those who
keep God's commandments and
stand up for Jesus.

Look!

The Great Red Dragon takes his stand
on the shore of the sea.

Interpretation: What does the text say?

The main characters of this dramatic vision are: the pregnant

Mother, the Dragon, the male child who is the Lamb of God, Michael and his angels, and the rest of the offspring of the Glorious Mother.

The place to begin the interpretation of chapter 12 is at the end. **The rest of** the **offspring** of the Glorious Mother are **those who keep the commandments of God and bear testimony to Jesus,** i.e., faithful Christians. They would include those **who have conquered** the dragon **by the blood of the Lamb of God and by the word of their testimony, who loved not their lives even unto death,** Christian martyrs (v. 11).

The Great Red Dragon is the persecutor of the faithful Christians (v. 17), and of the Glorious Mother (v. 13f). He is **the Devil, Satan, the deceiver of the whole world** (v. 9).

The male child is **caught up to God and to his throne.** He is **to rule the nations,** that is, he is the Messiah, the Lamb of God, the Christ (v. 5).

The Glorious Mother is the one from whom came forth the faithful Christians (v. 17), the martyrs (v. 11), and the Messiah (v. 5). She may be thought of in a collective sense as the Church, possibly including the people of God of the Old Testament as well. Mary, the mother of Jesus, is not intended. The details of the chapter do not fit her.

One of the outstanding features of chapter 12 and those that follow is that the eternal struggle between good and evil that has been lurking in the shadows now is brought out into the open and brought down to earth. The battle dramatically present in the birth of the male child is won in heaven with the victory of Michael and his angels. The Great Red Dragon, the Devil, is cast down to earth where he makes war against the church, those who do God's will and bear witness to Jesus (v. 17). The ultimate victory is not won until the Great Red Dragon and his cohorts are thrown into the lake of fire and brimstone (19:20; 20:10, 14-15).

The Message

That reader is wise who pays particular attention to what the voices in Revelation and especially the heavenly voices say. Verse 11 stands at the center of the chapter. A loud voice from heaven says, **They have conquered him** (the Devil) through the **blood of the Lamb** and through the saving purpose of God to which they bore witness **for they loved not their lives even unto death.**

The Christian's victory over evil is in the last analysis Christ's victory. It is won by his death. It has brought life to men. Salvation is a gift. Yet it can only be received and appropriated by faithfulness of the quality of which martyrdom is the chief example. The act of staking one's life on what one believes speaks far more loudly than one's words.

THE TWO MONSTERS   13:1-18

Introduction

Chapter 13 depicts the Great Red Dragon's war against the off-spring of the Woman. The war is waged not by the Dragon but by his two archdeputies on earth, the Vicious Monster who came up out of the sea and the Two-horned Lamb.

To picture the visions of chapter 13 calls on all the powers of our imagination. The Great Red Dragon stands on the seashore. Rising out of the sea comes the Vicious Monster with ten horns, seven heads and ten crowns. To the Vicious Monster the Great Red Dragon gives his throne, power and authority. When it comes closer we see that one of its heads seems mortally wounded but miraculously healed. Overwhelmed by the authority granted to the Vicious Monster, men worship it saying, "Who is like the Vicious Monster? Who can fight against it?"

For forty-two months the Vicious Monster is allowed to blaspheme against God, to exercise authority, and to make war and conquer the saints. All who dwell on earth save those whose names are written in the Lamb's book of life worship the Vicious Monster.

The Vision   13:1-10

See in your imagination the Sea Monster before going on to view the action that follows.
YOU ARE THERE!

Look!	John sees a monster rising out of the sea.	13:1
	It has seven heads and ten horns.	
	On the heads a name of blasphemy is written.	
Look!	The ten horns are crowned.	
	The Vicious Monster looks like a leopard and has feet like a bear's.	2
	His mouth is like a lion's mouth.	
Look!	To the Vicious Monster the Great Red Dragon gives his power, his throne, and his enormous authority.	
See!	One of its seven heads appears dead!	3

Look!	It has come back to life!
Look!	The whole world is amazed and falls under the spell of the Vicious Monster and worships the Vicious Monster and the Great Red Dragon.

Listen! The peoples are saying,
There is no one in all heaven, or earth, or under the earth who is like the Monster. Who is able to resist it?

Listen! For forty-two months the Vicious Monster blasphemes God himself and all who dwell in heaven.

Look! For forty-two months the Vicious Monster makes wars on the saints and overcomes them.

Look! It is given authority over every tribe and people and tongue and nation.

All earth-dwellers are worshiping it, that is, everyone whose name is not written in the Lamb's book of life.

Listen! *If you have ears that can hear, hear!"
Whoever is destined to be imprisoned, to prison he shall go; Whoever takes up the sword and kills, with the sword he shall be killed.*

Note this! Here is the meaning of it all: Be loyal! Stand fast! Keep the faith!

(verse numbers: 4, 5, 6, 7, 8, 9, 10)

Interpretation: What does the text say?

The function of the vision of the Sea Monster is to call Christians, **the saints,** to stand up against the Vicious Monster and his hosts with fortitude and to hold fast to their faith in the Lamb of God even unto death! Martyrdom seems to be a distinct possibility, for the Vicious Monster is permitted to conquer them (v. 7). In this war the Monster is carrying out the dastardly deeds of the Devil, the Great Red Dragon (v. 2). The Devil has given him his power, his authority, and even his throne (v. 2) so that he can carry out his wicked will.

Members of the seven churches of Asia would understand the

Vicious Monster to represent the Roman Empire for it has **authority** over the whole earth (vv. 7-8). In the first century the Roman Empire was understood to be the "world." America and other lands had not yet been discovered. The seven heads may represent emperors and the ten horns provincial officials. The numbers, seven and ten, are symbolical of fullness or completeness rather than of precise numerical significance.

Note that the earth-dwellers worship the Great Red Dragon, i.e., the Devil, and the Vicious Monster, the Roman Empire and the emperors (vv. 4, 8).

The Vicious Monster bears a blasphemous name on its heads. In the last analysis blasphemy is the usurping of the prerogatives of God. It is the violation of the first commandment — "Thou shalt have no other Gods before me." The emperor Domitian demanded to be addressed as "Lord" and "God." Other emperors accepted divine titles and at times worship. Divine titles such as *divus* (divine) appeared on Roman coins. In inscriptions the terms *theos* (god) and *huios theou* (son of god) were applied to Roman emperors.

Forty-two months is a short time, the time the Roman Empire is permitted to exercise authority and persecute God's people.

The first part of verse 10 is a word of advice for the persecuted, "Don't resist; resistance will be futile." The second part is a challenge to the conqueror and a comfort to the persecuted. It may be a paraphrase of the word of Jesus, "They who take the sword shall perish by the sword."

The head that apparently had been killed but later **its "mortal wound" was healed** could well refer to an emperor who had died but of whom the rumor arose that he was alive and would return to the throne. This would be similar to the rumor that circulated about Adolph Hitler after World War II. The Roman historians Tacitus and Suetonius report such a rumor about Nero. After Nero committed suicide in A.D. 68, the rumor arose that he was not dead but had gone into hiding in Parthia and that he would return at the head of a vast Parthian army to devastate Rome. In time the rumor developed into the belief that he had died but would be resurrected.

THE TWO-HORNED LAMB   13:11-18

Introduction

A second beast, two-horned, arises out of the earth. While it looks like a lamb, it speaks like the Great Red Dragon. The Two-horned Lamb exercises all the authority of the Vicious Monster. It compels the earth and its inhabitants to worship the Monster whose wound was healed. By making fire come down from heaven, the Two-horned Lamb deceives men into fashioning an image of the Vicious Monster, gives breath to the image, compels all to worship it, and slays those who refuse. Everyone, rich and poor, slave and free, is required to be branded on the hand or forehead with the mark of the Vicious Monster or the number of its name in order to buy or sell. The number of the Vicious Monster is 666!

Vision   13:11-18
YOU ARE THERE!

Look!	The second beast comes out of the earth.	13:11
	It has two horns like a lamb but speaks like the Great Red Dragon.	
Listen to it!	*All you who dwell on earth, worship the Vicious Monster for he has been resurrected.*	12
Look!	Fire is coming down from heaven.	13
	The Two-horned Lamb is working a miracle.	
Listen!	He commands,	14
	Build an image of the Vicious Monster whose mortal wound was healed!	
Look!	He is allowed to breathe the breath of life into the image of the Vicious Monster so that it speaks.	15
Listen to the command of the Two-horned Lamb!		
	Bow down before the image of the Vicious Monster!	
Look!	Earth-dwellers are bowing down to the idol of the Vicious Monster. Those refusing to worship his image are being killed.	
Look!	Only those who bear the brand of the Vicious Monster or the number of its name on the right hand or forehead are permitted to buy or sell.	17
Note this!	The number of the Vicious Monster is a human number. Its number is 666!	18

Interpretation: What does the text say?

What is the identity of beast that comes out of the earth? Note its appearance, its relationships, and its function. This second beast looks like a two-horned lamb. This is an obvious contrast to the Lamb of God, the redeemer of the saints. The Two-horned Lamb speaks like the Great Red Dragon, the Devil. Just like the Monster exercised the authority of the Great Red Dragon, so the Two-horned Lamb exercises the authority of the Vicious Monster. The Great Red Dragon and the Two-horned Lamb belong together. With the Vicious Monster, they form a kind of "unholy trinity."

The chief functions of the Two-horned Lamb are related to worship. It **makes the earth and its inhabitants worship** the Vicious Monster. It works miracles: it makes **fire come down from heaven,** it gives **breath to the image of the Monster.** It causes an idol of the Vicious Monster to be built and those who will not bow down to the idol to be slain. It also carries out economic sanctions against those who refuse to worship the Monster (v. 17). Religion, politics, and economics were closely related in the Roman Empire. Refusal to worship the emperor could have serious economic consequences.

If the Vicious Monster represents the Roman Empire and its heads Roman emperors, then the Two-horned Lamb represents the officials who make the people worship the emperor and the goddess Roma.

The meaning of the number 666 is disputed. Since it is connected with the Vicious Monster and is a **human number,** it probably refers to one of the Roman emperors. Greek and Hebrew did not have a separate system of numbers. Instead they used letters of the alphabet to represent numbers. One of the most plausible interpretations is based on the fact that if Nero Caesar is written in Hebrew letters, the numerical total would be 666.

Nero persecuted the Christians in Rome. He blamed the burning of Rome on them though it is thought that he himself started the conflagration. He is said to have used Christians as torches in his gardens.

Message

Nowhere else in the book of Revelation is the demonic character of evil so clearly spelled out. John's thought pictures a hierarchy of evil which opposes and attempts to conquer the hierarchy of good. The two hierarchies may be represented thus:

The Hierarchy of Good	The Hierarchy of Evil
God	The Devil
The Lamb (Christ)	His Deputies on Earth:
	The Monster from the Sea
	The Two-horned Lamb
	(Known in 16:13 as the False
	Prophet)
The saints (v. 7)	The earth-dwellers (vv. 3, 8, 12,
	and 16) "all" who bear the
	brand of the Monster

The two hierarchies are locked in mortal combat. The hierarchy of evil wars on the saints and conquers them. Captivity and martyrdom are to be expected as part of the cost of being a Christian. This calls for courageous fortitude, for a heroic faith that enables persons to stand anything that could happen to them (v. 10).

Nowhere is the demonic character of evil so clearly seen as when it is interwoven with the structures of society. When industrial corporations become corrupt by the usurpation of power then the system rides roughshod over the rights of people and becomes beastly. Minorities, and the "little people" suffer the most. Civil power becomes the expression of evil. Politicians in grasping for power tend to become a law unto themselves. Presidents declare themselves to be above the law and assume to themselves absolute power and authority, the very prerogatives of Almighty God. Truth is nailed to the cross and deception ascends the throne. Persecution by FBI, CIA, departments of the government, and minor "bull frogs" in the political pond becomes all too common.

The powerful politician demands and rewards absolute political loyalty. In such circumstances religion tends to become either the handmaiden of the state, i.e., "civil religion," or the object of persecution and even death. Nationalism becomes "man's other religion." Wars become crusades for "freedom," and "humanity," for "God" and country.

Perhaps the most notable example in modern times is that of Adolf Hitler and Nazi Germany. Hitler by force and deception ascended to power. His grasp for absolute power and authority was reinforced by the adulation of his followers. The entire movement took on a political, ethical, and religious character.

The common greeting accorded Adolf Hitler by fanatical hosts of Germans was *"Heil, Hitler."* Literally translated this means, "Salvation

Hitler." Hitler was regarded as the embodiment and the savior of the
German people. Men and women would tell with tears in their eyes of
the wonderful things Adolf Hitler did for them and for Germany.

When Hitler and his "German Christian" party tried to take over
the church, the "Confessing Church" was organized in opposition. It
was forced underground. Pastors were dismissed from their churches.
Some were thrown into concentration camps. Not a few were martyred.

The "German Christian" party planned to throw out the Old
Testament and revise the New to accord with their political beliefs.
They replaced the traditional creed, "One Lord, one faith, one bap-
tism" with "one Nation, one Folk, one Fuehrer!" and sang "Germany is
our honor, Germany is our glory. We will fight for Germany!"

American Christians tend to forget that suffering and tribulation
was a part of the church from the very beginning. Jesus was crucified;
Stephen, martyred. Paul was lashed with a whip and driven from place
to place. Silas was imprisoned; Niemoeller, persecuted; and Bonhoeffer
put to death in a concentration camp.

The call to the church is to remain steadfast, to keep the faith in
the face of the totalitarianism of nation, civil religion, economic giants,
and the military-industrial complex. Opposition, discrimination, hostil-
ity, suffering, and even persecution are to be expected by faithful followers of the Crucified Lamb of God.

---

1. This term is used by Adela Y. Collins, *The Combat Myth of the Book of
Revelation.* Scholars Press, 1976.

8
The Harvests
14:1-20

With chapter 14 we come to the end of the interlude between the seventh trumpet and the terrible plagues of the seven bowls.

The interlude began as a kind of "re-run" of the spiritual battle between the forces of good and the hosts of evil. The Devil thrown out of heaven came down to deceive the earth-dwellers and persecute the church. But never fear. The saints who remain steadfast and keep the faith (13:10) will triumph (14:1-5). The followers of the Great Red Dragon and his earthly counterparts, the Vicious Monster and the Two-horned Lamb must drink the wine of God's wrath and be tormented with fire and brimstone (14:10). So the interlude is brought to a satisfying, triumphant and just end.

In chapter 14 we see first the vision of the 144,000 redeemed on Mount Zion, then three angels making proclamations as they fly through mid-heaven, and finally two visions of judgment.

THE 144,000 ON MOUNT ZION   14:1-5

Introduction

The Lamb of God and with him 144,000 who have his name and the name of his Father written on their foreheads are standing on Mount Zion. The vast chorus of 144,000 sing as with one voice a new song composed for them alone. The singing sounds like the sound of many waters, like the sound of thunder, like the sound of harpers playing on their harps in God's court in heaven. They sing before the throne in the presence of the Elders and the Four Living Creatures.

The Vision   14:1-5
YOU ARE THERE!
Look!   The Lamb of God is standing on Mount   14:1

	Zion. With him are the 144,000	
	His name and the name of his Father are written on their foreheads.	
Listen to the voice from heaven!		
Hear!	The sound of many waters.	2
	Peals of thunder.	
	The sound of harpers playing on their harps.	
	144,000 redeemed from the earth singing a new song before the throne of God, before the Four Living Creatures, and before the Twenty-four Elders.	3
Note this!	These are the pure, who follow the Lamb wherever he goes.	4
	These are the redeemed, the first fruits for God and the Lamb.	
	They are blameless; no lie is in their mouth.	5

Interpretation: What does the text say?

As is characteristic of Revelation, the anticipatory vision of triumph comes before the vision of judgment. In the last analysis, heaven is always in control. No matter how bitter the struggle, in the end the saints overcome through the blood of the Lamb of God and worship before the throne of God.

The **Lamb** standing **on Mount Zion** with the **144,000 who had his name and his Father's name written on their foreheads** is the counterpart to the Vicious Monster and the Two-horned Lamb.

Deception is the chief means by which the Monster and the Two-horned Lamb gain their power. The seeming miracle of a fake resurrection (One head of the Vicious Monster **seemed to have a mortal wound but its wound was healed.**) deceives the earth-dwellers. It gets the **whole earth** to follow it with wonder and to worship. The similarity to the true **Lamb of God standing as though it had been slain** is apparent (5:6), but the resurrection of the true Lamb of God was no fake. He had been **slain** (5:9) but now was **alive for evermore** (1:18; 2:8). No doubt the Two-horned Lamb deceived the earth-dwellers because he bore apparent resemblance to the true Lamb of God.

The saints conquered by the Monster and possibly martyred (13:7-8) are not deceived. Now they are victorious for they have been **redeemed from mankind as first fruits for God and the Lamb** (14:4).

THE THREE FLYING ANGELS 14:6-13

Introduction

In sequence three angels fly in midheaven proclaiming God's message to every nation, tribe, tongue, and people. The first proclaims the Gospel with a voice loud enough for all the earth to hear, "Fear God and give him glory, for the hour of his judgment has come; worship him who made heaven and earth, the sea and the fountains of water."

The second angel follows crying, "Fallen, fallen is Babylon the great, who made the nations drink the wine of her impure passions."

The third angel cries, "If anyone worships the Vicious Monster and its image and receives a mark on his forehead or on his hand, he shall drink the wine of God's wrath, poured unmixed into the cup of his anger, and he shall be tormented with fire and brimstone in the presence of the holy angels and in the presence of the Lamb."

The Vision 14:6-13
YOU ARE THERE!

Look!	Another angel flying in mid-heaven is proclaiming an eternal Gospel to those who dwell on the earth, to every nation and tribe and tongue and people.	14:6
Now Hear This!		
	Fear God and give him glory for the hour of his judgment has come.	7
	Worship the maker of heaven and earth, the sea and the springs of water!	
Look!	A second angel follows crying, *Fallen, fallen is Babylon the great, who made all nations drink the wine of her impure passion.*	8
Look!	A third angel follows them shouting,	9
Listen!	*Whoever worships the Vicious Monster and its image and is branded with its mark on his forehead or on his hand shall drink the wine of God's wrath poured unmixed into the cup of his anger, and shall be tortured with fire and brimstone in the presence of the holy angels and the Lamb of God.*	10

Look!   The smoke of their torment goes up for   11
ever and ever.
They have no rest, day or night, those
worshipers of the Vicious Monster
and its image, who bear the brand
of the Monster.

Now Hear This!

Here is the meaning of it all: be loyal;   12
stand fast!
All God's people, keep the com-
mandments of God and the faith in
Jesus!

Listen!   A voice from heaven commands John,   13
Write this, Blessed are the dead
who from this time on die as Chris-
tians.

Listen!   The Spirit says,
I guarantee it.
They shall rest from their labors for
their deeds accompany them.

Interpretation: What does the text say?

The author himself tells us what the basic meaning of the passage is. **Here is a call for the patient endurance of the saints.** "Saints" are defined as **those who keep the commandments of God and** their **faith in Jesus** in the face of the persecution by the Vicious Monster and the Two-horned Lamb, i.e., the political and religious authorities of the Roman Empire (ch. 13). Those who will face martyrdom are especially in mind (14:13). They are promised "rest" as the reward for their deeds.

The proclamation of the first flying angel is a call to repentance addressed to all earth-dwellers and an announcement that **the hour of judgment has come.** The end-time is here. **Fear God, give him glory, worship** the creator of **heaven and earth, the sea and the fountains of water** (14:7).

The second flying angel proclaims the doom of **Babylon.** She is identified as the power who made all nations commit immorality, i.e., worship false gods. The members of the seven churches would understand this to refer to the Roman Empire, specifically involving emperor worship and the worship of the goddess Roma.

The third flying angel warns earth-dwellers against worshiping the Vicious Monster, i.e., Rome, and proclaims the doom of those who do not repent. They shall **drink the unmixed wine of God's wrath.** The ultimate punishment is described as continual **torment** by **fire and brimstone.**

THE HARVEST OF GRAIN   14:14-16

Introduction

    The action takes place on the gigantic stage of heaven and earth. We see seated on a white cloud one like a son of man wearing a crown of gold and carrying a tremendous sickle large enough to reap the earth. An angel comes out of the temple calling with a loud voice to the son of man, "Put in your sickle and reap, for the harvest is fully ripe and the hour to reap has come!" With one tremendous sweep of his sickle the grain harvest of the entire earth is reaped.

The Vision   14:14-16
YOU ARE THERE!

Look!	A white cloud! Seated on the cloud is one who looks like a son of man.	14:14
	A crown of gold is on his head, and a sharp sickle is in his hand.	
Look!	Another angel comes from the temple.	15
Listen!	He calls loudly to the one who has the sickle, *Swing your sickle, Reap the harvest. It is fully ripe, and the harvest time is here!*	
Look!	The one sitting on the cloud swings his enormous sickle.	16
	With one swing the earth is reaped.	

THE GREAT WINE PRESS   14:17-20

Introduction

    The grain harvest is followed by the ingathering of vintage of the entire earth. The method of harvest is unusual. The grapes are not plucked from the vine. Instead one sweep of an enormous sickle reaps the world's crop. The grapes are then processed by treading them out in the vast wine press of God's wrath. Blood flows from the wine press in a flood as high as a horse's bridle for two hundred miles.

    The entire process, as is usual in Revelation, is directed from heaven. It is carried out by angels, the first from the temple in heaven, the second from the altar of God.

The Vision   14:17-20
YOU ARE THERE!

Look!	Another angel comes out of the temple. 14:17
	He, too, has a sharp sickle.
Over There!	From the altar comes the angel who has 18
	power over fire.
Listen!	He shouts to the angel with the sharp
	sickle,
	Use your sickle to gather grapes
	from the earth's vineyards, for the
	grapes are ripe.
Look!	With one sweep of his sickle the angel 19
	cuts the grapes from the vine, and
	throws them into the great
	winepress of God's wrath.
Look!	The winepress is trodden outside the 20
	city's walls.
	Blood flows from the wine press as high
	as a horse's bridle for two hundred
	miles.

Interpretation: What does the text say?

These are judgment scenes.

The grain is harvested by one **like a son of man.** This probably means by the heavenly Christ since the phrase was used of the resurrected Christ in chapter 1. Furthermore the reaper is obviously not an angel. The command, "Reap!" is from God. The angel is his messenger. Christ wears the crown, a symbol of sovereignty and possibly victory (See 2:10).

The basic problem here is to what does the symbol of the harvest refer. It is plausible that it refers to the harvest of the righteous for the following reasons. The 144,000 redeemed are said to be **the first fruits,** i.e., of the redeemed. Other fruit must have been expected. The call to repentance and **worship** is connected with **the hour of his judgment** and could possibly have borne fruit (v. 7). G. B. Caird, in his commentary on Revelation, points out that the Greek words *therismos* (a harvest) and *therizo* (harvesting) in the Gospels are used of gathering people into the kingdom of God. Even in the Greek Old Testament, these words are not used of mowing down enemies. The vision of the grape picking (vv. 17-20), on the other hand, portrays judgment of the wicked. The enormous crop of grapes is trodden under foot in the wine press of God's wrath. From the wine press flows a river of **blood high as a horse's bridle,** two hundred miles long! This almost defies the powers

of the imagination. Earlier in the chapter the third angel proclaims that
the wicked shall drink the wine of God's wrath . . . unmixed.

Here, in chapters 12-14, we have come full circle from the beginning. The birth of the Messiah and heaven's victory over the Devil in
chapter 12 is followed by the persecution of the church by the Roman
emperors and their cohorts in chapter 13 and the judgment in chapter
14. The final outcome is foreshadowed by the victory of the Lamb and
the 144,000 on Mount Zion. It is carried out in the grain and grape
harvests. The earth-dwellers, those who worship the Monster, must inevitably drink **the wine of God's wrath** which is **poured out unmixed**
into the cup of his anger.

The destruction of the wicked is pictured in other imagery in
chapters 19 and 20.

Message

The blessedness of those who die in the Lord and especially of those
who become martyrs is in stark contrast to the unspeakable horror of the
judgment on the wicked. The memorial service of a Christian is a celebration, albeit through tears, of the new life ahead before the throne of
God, of the singing of the song of Moses and of the Lamb on the one
hand and the celebration of their life stories on the other. **For their
deeds follow them!**

The law of the harvest is a favorite biblical theme. We reap what we
sow. There is a bent to the universe. Those who go against the grain must
pay the consequences. In this sense also their deeds follow them.
John would go further and say their non-deeds follow them. If persons do
not give glory to God and worship the creator of heaven and earth, the sea
and the fountains of water, the judgment of God will be upon them.

What is more damnable still is compelling others to do evil, making
all nations drink the wine of her impure passion. Their condemna-
tion is inevitable and just.

Nevertheless in the very hour when judgment falls, the opportunity
for repentance and salvation is available to all. Often **the eternal
gospel,** the great invitation to repent, **to fear God and give him glory,**
sounds most clearly and poignantly in the imminence of crisis.

It is in such crises also that courage is demanded, that the clarion
call to heroism rings the loudest, that the saints are summoned to hold
fast to the end, to **keep the commandments of God and the faith of
Jesus.**

In the time of crisis there is a kind of black and white to moral deci-

82 VISIONS OF GLORY

sion. Society tends to muddy the waters, to rationalize, to move toward compromise. But in the last analysis there comes a time when "the buck stops here." When the decision cannot be put off, that decision takes on a kind of absolute quality.

Moreover moral decisions, although influenced by numerous forces—many of them beyond the control of the decider, are finally individual decisions. The individual must take the responsibility and shoulder the consequence.

The Message of Chapters 12-14

The great themes of Revelation are blown up to gigantic proportions in the interlude 12-14. The tremendous spiritual conflict between Good and Evil, between God and the Devil, becomes an ever-present reality for the seven churches. It becomes embodied in their daily life as they struggle to keep the faith. Pressured by fellow workers to participate in idol feasts, seduced by false teachers, compelled at times by over-patriotic officials to worship the Roman state and emperor, the saints become hard put to it to keep the commandments of God. John sees that the struggle is real. Some will have to face the existential choice, "Worship the emperor, or die!"

But the victory is sure! It has already been won in heaven. It is just as certain that it will be won on earth. Caesar and his deputies will rule for a short while. But their end is coming!

Justice will be done! The wicked will be punished! The emperor and those who refuse to repent will drink the wine of God's wrath unmixed and have not rest day or night.

To the true people of God the message is clear. Never fear! God is in control. Try as he did, Satan could not snatch the newborn babe; he could not destroy the Messiah. The babe was caught up to God's throne. The forces of evil are trying to destroy the Church. But never fear! The Church will endure. She is under the protection of God. The Glorious Mother was given wings of an eagle and a place of safety in the desert.

The challenge to Christians is also clear. Don't let patriotism become your religion. Remain steadfast in the face of political, economic, social, and religious pressures. Do not compromise. Hold fast to your faith in God and in Christ—even in the face of martyrdom! Give God the glory, not Caesar! Worship God, not the state. Keep his commandments. Your reward is sure. Blessed are the dead who die in the Lord. Your righteous deeds will follow you. You will find God's rest from your trials.

9
Seven Bowls of Wrath
15:1—16:21

The section of the book from 15:1—19:21 may be entitled "The Victory Over Babylon." It includes a new series of judgments unfolding the wrath of God and the celebration of victory. Victory and the wrath are two sides of the same coin. Both were announced by flying angels in chapter 14. Drinking the wine of God's wrath is to be the lot of everyone who worships the Vicious Monster and its image and receives its brand on the forehead or hand (14:9).

There are four segments in this section: the seven bowls of wrath (15:1—16:21), an appendix detailing the fall of Babylon (17:1—18:24), the victory celebration (19:1-10), and the final battle (19:11—21).

The section works up in a crescendo of intensity not seen before until Babylon falls, the saints in heaven shout "Hallelujah!" and the final battle is won by the Word of God.

THE SEVEN BOWLS OF WRATH   15:1—16:21

Introduction

The setting again is heaven. The redeemed, those who have conquered the Vicious Monster and understand the number of its name, are standing beside the sea of glass. It is a worship scene. The redeemed have harps of God in their hands and sing the song of Moses and the Lamb. The setting differs from the throne room scenes (4; 5; 7:9—9:17; 11:15-19). Instead of the throne we have the "temple of the tabernacle." Seven angels robed in pure bright linen come out of the temple. They are given the seven golden bowls full of the wrath of God. The temple is filled with the smoke of the glory of God and his power.

The angels are commanded by a voice from the temple to go and pour out the bowls of the wrath of God upon the earth.

The Vision   15:1 — 16:21
YOU ARE THERE!

Look!	Another great and amazing omen in heaven, seven angels with seven plagues, which are the last.	15:1
	With them the wrath of God is ended.	
Look!	A sea of glass mingled with fire! Standing at the sea of glass with harps of God in their hands are the victors over the Monster and its idol and the number of its name.	2
	As they play the harps they sing the song of Moses, God's slave, and the song of the Lamb,	3
Listen!	*Great and marvelous are your works, Lord God the Almighty!*	
	Just and trustworthy are your ways, King of the ages!	
	Who will not fear and glorify your name for you alone are holy?	4
	All nations will come and worship you for the justice of your sentence is now clear.	

YOU ARE THERE!

Look!	The temple, that is, the tent of testimony in heaven, is thrown open!	5
	Out come seven angels robed in pure shining linen with gold scarves around their shoulders.	6
Look!	One of the Four Living Creatures gives the seven angels seven golden bowls full of the wrath of God who lives forever.	7
Look!	The temple bellows with smoke from the glory of God and his power so that no one can enter the temple until the seven plagues of the seven angels is ended.	8
Listen!	From the sanctuary comes a loud voice commanding the seven angels:	16:1
	Go and pour out the seven bowls of God's wrath on the earth!	

Look!   So the first angel goes and pours his   2
bowl of wrath on the earth. Foul
and evil ulcers break out on those
who bear the monster's brand and
worship its statue.

Look!   The second angel pours his bowl into   3
the sea.
It turns to blood, like the blood of a
dead person. Everything in the sea
dies.

Look!   The third angel pours his bowl into the   4
rivers and springs.
They turn to blood.

Look!   Then we see the angel of the water and   5
hear him say,

Listen!   *You are just in your verdicts and their
execution, O Holy One, Who Is and
Who Was.*
    They have shed the blood of God's   6
*people and of prophets, so you
have given them blood to drink.*
    *They are getting what they de-
serve.*

Hark!   Then the altar cries,   7
    *Yes, Lord God the All-powerful,
true and just are your judgments!*

Look!   The fourth angel pours his bowl on the   8
sun.
The sun scorches men and women with   9
fire.

Listen!   They cry out in anguish because of the
fierce heat and curse God who has
power over these plagues.

Note this!   But they do not repent or give God glory.

Look!   The fifth angel pours his bowl on the   10
throne of the Monster.
Darkness falls on his kingdom.
His subjects gnaw their tongues because of the pain and curse the   11
God of heaven for their pain and
ulcers.
But they will not repent of their evil
deeds.

Look!   The sixth angel pours his bowl on the   12
                   mighty Euphrates River.
                   In an instant the river dries up to provide
                   a highway for the eastern kings.

Look!   Three foul spirits that look like frogs   13
                   come out of the mouth of the Red
                   Dragon and out of the mouth of
                   the Monster and out of the mouth
                   of the False Prophet.

                   They are demonic spirits who perform   14
                   miracles, sent abroad to the kings
                   of the whole world to muster them
                   for battle on the Great Day of God
                   the All-powerful.

Attention!   *I am coming like a thief in the darkness*   15
                   of night.
                   Fortunate is he who stays awake and
                   dressed so that he will not have to
                   walk around nude and be stared at.

Look!   They are mustering the troops at Arma-   16
                   geddon!

Look!   The seventh angel pours his bowl into   17
                   the air.

Listen!   A loud voice comes out of the temple
                   from the throne,
                   It is done!

Look! Listen! Lightning flashes,   18
                   thunder rumbles and crashes
                   and a tremendous earthquake
                   breaks the Richter scale!

Look!   The Great City splits into three pieces!   19
Note this!   God does not forget Babylon the Great.
                   He makes her drain the cup of fury
                   of his wrath to the last drop.

Look!   Every island flees and vanishes!   20
                   Not one mountain can be found!

                   Huge hailstones of tremendous weight   21
                   fall from heaven on mankind.

Listen!   Men curse God because the plague of
                   the hail is so terrible.

Interpretation: What does the text say?
    Verse 1 must mean that this is the last series of **plagues** depicting

the wrath of God. After this series of the **bowls** of **the wrath of God** it still remains for the Vicious Monster, the False Prophet (the Two-horned Lamb), Satan (the Great Red Dragon), Death and Hades to be thrown into the Lake of Fire (19:20; 20:10, 14).

This is the third series of seven plagues. In the first group, the seven seals, destruction was limited to one-fourth of the earth (6:8). The coming of **the great day of the wrath of** God and **of the Lamb** was announced (6:17). In the second series, the seven trumpets, destruction increased to one-third, but there was still opportunity to repent (9:20). In this third series of seven plagues, the **golden bowls of God's wrath,** there is one last opportunity to repent (16:11). However, the intensification is complete and **with them the wrath of God is ended** (15:1).

Each of the series included a preparatory event. The worship services in the throne room in heaven (chs. 4-5) provided the setting for the opening of the seven seals. The trumpet series was introduced by half an hour of silence and prayers of the saints for justice (cf. 8:4 with 6:10). Here in the bowl series, the souls of the martyrs are no longer under the altar but already **have conquered** the Vicious Monster (15:2) and are singing in celebrative worship the song of Moses and the Lamb (15:2-3). In his characteristic way, the author again reassures the members of the seven churches in Asia beforehand that no matter how terrible the plagues, in the end the saints will come through victorious. What is more, God and the Lamb are in control of history and eternity!

All nations shall come and worship thee (v. 4) taken out of context could be understood as proclaiming universal salvation. However, the clear statement of many verses in Revelation is that there are people who refuse to repent (cf. 9:20, 21; 11:18; 16:10; 2:21). There is a synagogue of Satan (2:9). There are people who worship the Great Red Dragon and the Vicious Monster and persecute the saints (13:4). Thus all nations must mean "some people from everywhere."

The plagues of the bowls of wrath, more than those of the seven trumpets are reminiscent of the plagues in Exodus. The mention of the **Song of Moses** reinforces this relationship. As Moses delivered the children of Israel from Egypt so the new Moses, the Lamb, has redeemed the saints and freed them from bondage to the Vicious Monster. In fact, the saints by their martyrdom have conquered him (15:2).

God's presence here is indicated not by the throne as in chapters 4 and 5 but by **the heavenly temple** and the **tent of witness,** i.e., the heavenly counterpart of the tabernacle used as God's dwelling in the

Sinai wilderness wanderings. The judgment plagues emanate from God and are carried out by his angels. The **smoke from the glory of God** (15:8) is analagous to the cloud by day and the pillar of fire by night that represented the presence of God in the Mosaic wilderness wanderings.

Here the first plague directly affects persons in contrast to the plague of the first trumpet which essentially wrought destruction on the natural world. Judgment on those who bear the brand of the Monster and worship him is intensifying. **Every living thing in the sea** dies (16:3). All the **rivers and fountains of water** become **blood** (16:4). Total **darkness** engulfs the kingdom of the Monster (16:10). The cry of the **altar, "Yea, Lord God the Almighty, true and just are thy judgments!"** may be in response to the cry of the martyrs under the altar in 6:10.

The fifth bowl of wrath is poured on the throne of the Vicious Monster, the very heart of his kingdom, but not even that brings the earth-dwellers to repent. Instead they **curse the God of heaven for their pain and their sores** (16:11).

The sixth bowl contemplates a great final eschatological battle between the forces of evil and the forces of good. The former would include the Devil (the Great Red Dagon), the Vicious Monster, and the False Prophet (Two-horned Lamb). For the members of the seven churches, these would be the political and religious leaders of the Roman Empire, i.e., the emperor and those in charge of the worship of the emperor and the goddess Roma. To these would be added the kings of all the earth-dwellers and their armies. Apparently God the Almighty is more than able to handle the other side. At least none of his cohorts are mentioned (16:12-14).

The place of the eschatological battle is called Armageddon (16:16). Although this is mentioned only in one verse in Revelation it has evoked all kinds of speculation. The Hebrew term probably means *The Mountain of Megiddo*. Megiddo was a strong fortress guarding the pass into the plain of Esdraelon which is also called "the Plain of Megiddo" by St. Jerome. It would be impossible in any literal sense to assemble all the armies of the world in such a small place. The best solution is to realize that John is portraying a vision and that Armageddon is a symbol representing the final decisive battle between good and evil, between God and the Devil.

Verse 15 is another verse meant by John to motivate and encourage the members of the seven churches to keep the faith. Stay awake! Be prepared!

Like the sixth seal and the seventh trumpet, the seventh bowl depicts the end. **The voice from the temple, from the throne,** i.e., God's voice, proclaims the end, It is done! The downfall of the great persecutor of the church, Babylon, i.e., Rome and the Roman Empire, and of the worshipers of the Vicious Monster (Rome) as predicted in 14:8 and 10 is accomplished. In the Bible, God often uses natural phenomena in making known his presence and carrying out his will. Here in accomplishing the fall of Babylon (the Roman Empire) there is an earthquake that "out-earthquakes" all other earthquakes. **The great city is split into three parts,** the empire crumbles (the cities of the nations will fall) and Babylon is made to **drain** the last drop from **the cup of God's wrath.** Babylon is finished!

The details of the fall of Babylon, the great persecutor of the church and the final battle will be spelled out later.

Message

Chapter 15 proclaims the greatness of God. He alone is all powerful as his marvelous deeds demonstrate. He is just and true. He is "King of the ages!" He is worthy of the worship of all peoples! Everyone should stand in awe of him and glorify his person!

The wrath of God is not a subject about which people like to hear. Yet it is one of the dominant subjects of the book of Revelation. It means "the divine reaction against evil." It involves judgment and, in the thought of the author of Revelation, punishment for evil doing.

God's wrath is an essential part of his character. John would see it as including more than the inevitable, impersonal consequence of evil doing. If God is active in doing good in carrying out his saving work, he is also active in the judgment on and punishing of evil. The loud voice from the temple, i.e., from God, gives the order to the seven angels to pour their bowls of his wrath on the Vicious Monster and his followers. The Russian hymn has it right. "God the all-terrible! King who ordainest thunder Thy clarion, the lightning Thy sword. . . . " The all-terrible evil in this world can only be defeated by the all-terrible God. God did not forget Babylon!

The purpose of God's judgment on persons in the immediate situation is repentance and salvation. In the end-time it is the complete destruction of evil.

The very real danger is that the perversity of persons will lead them to respond with curses and self-justification rather than with repentance.

This is similar to the sin against the Holy Spirit of which Jesus spoke. If one continues to refuse to respond to the voice of the Spirit speaking to one's heart and conscience, there may come a time when one can no longer hear the Spirit speaking. Repentance then becomes no longer possible. A person will reap what he/she sows. Judgment is inevitable.

10

Babylon and Her Fall
17:1—18:24

The next chapters are an important appendix to the seven bowls of God's wrath. The fall of "Babylon" announced by the flying angel (14:8) and accomplished in the sixth bowl ("It is done!" 16:17) is detailed in 17:1—19:21.

The section may be divided into four parts.

1. Babylon, the Great Prostitute (17)
2. Funeral Dirge Over Babylon (18)
3. The Victory Celebration in Heaven (19:1-10)
4. The Great Supper of God (19:11-21)

One might expect the book of Revelation to end here with the final victory of Christ and of God over "Babylon" (Rome) portrayed as the Vicious Monster and the False Prophet. They are thrown alive into the lake of fire (19:20). However behind the Monster and the False Prophet stands the Great Red Dragon (Satan) lurking in the shadows. Behind the visible earthly struggle between the people of God and the empire lies the unseen spiritual struggle between God (good) and Satan (evil).

The remaining chapters (20-22) are given over to the final victory of heaven (God) over the Devil and the depiction of the New Heaven and New Earth, the reward of the righteous.

BABYLON, THE GREAT PROSTITUTE   17:1-18

Introduction

Chapter 17 is divided between the repulsive vision of the Great Prostitute and the Monster in verses 1-6 and the interpretation of the vision by the angel in verses 7-18.

Again, essential to a meaningful understanding of this passage is the experience of seeing the vision in your imagination.

An angel carries John away in the Spirit into a wilderness. There he

sees the Great Prostitute sitting on a scarlet Monster, which was full of
names of blasphemy. The Monster has seven heads and ten horns. The
Prostitute is arrayed as a queen in purple and scarlet and is decked out
in jewels, gold and pearls. In her hand she holds a golden cup full of
abominations. On her forehead is written a name of mystery, "Babylon
the Great, Mother of Prostitutes." She is drunk with the blood of the
saints and the blood of the martyrs of Jesus.

In the remainder of the chapter, the angel explains to John the
mystery of the Great Prostitute and the Monster. The Great Prostitute is
the great city which has dominion over the kings of the earth. The water
on which she is seated are peoples and multitudes, nations, and tongues.
The Monster and his cohorts are those who will war on the Lamb, but
the Lamb will conquer them.

The Vision   17:1-18
YOU ARE THERE!

Look!	One of the seven angels who had the seven bowls of God's wrath comes.	17:1
Listen!	He says to John, *Come, I will show you the doom of the Great Prostitute who is sitting on many waters.*	
	The kings of the earth have committed adultery with her. She has made the earth-dwellers drunk with the wine of her prostitution.	2
Look!	John is whisked away in the Spirit to a desert.	3
Look!	A woman enthroned upon a scarlet Monster with blasphemous names written all over it! It has seven heads and ten horns.	
Look!	She is dressed as a queen, in purple and scarlet, glittering with gold, jewels, and pearls.	4
Look!	In her hand she holds a gold cup full of obscenities and the filth of her whoredom.	
Note this!	On her forehead is written a mysterious name, *Babylon the Great, Mother of Prostitutes and Obscenities.*	5

And this!   She is drunk with the blood of God's   6
people and the blood of those mar-
tyred for the sake of Jesus.

Listen to the angel!

Why are you amazed, John?   7
*I will tell you the meaning of the
woman and of the Monster with
seven heads and ten horns.*

Listen!   *The Monster that you saw was alive*   8
*once, but lives no longer, is about
to ascend from the bottomless
abyss and go forth to destruction.*

Look!   The earth-dwellers whose names are
not written in the Book of Life are
amazed to see the Monster reappear
because it was alive once, and then died!
A wise man can decipher this!   9

Note this!   *The seven heads are seven hills on which
the woman sits enthroned. They are*   10
*also seven kings: five have fallen,
one still rules, the other is still to
come. When he comes his rule will
be brief.*

The Monster who lived and lives no more   11
*is an eighth but belongs to the seven
and goes to destruction.*

The ten horns are ten kings who have not   12
yet received their kingdoms.
*Together with the Monster they will
reign as kings for one hour.*

They will give their power to the   13
Monster and wage war on the   14
Lamb;
*but the Lamb will conquer them for he is
Lord of lords and King of kings.
His followers are called, elected,
and loyal.*

Listen to the Interpreting Angel!

The waters that you see on which the   15
*Great Prostitute is enthroned are
peoples and nations and tongues.*

The ten horns and the Monster will hate   16
*the prostitute; they will strip her and
make her naked, they will eat her*

flesh and burn up the remains in
fire.
For God has put it into their heads to   17
carry out his purpose
by giving over their kingdom to the
Monster until God's plan is completely carried out.
The woman that you see is the great   18
city that rules over all the kingdoms
of the earth.

Interpretation: What does the text say?

As we have seen, the way to be on firm ground in interpreting
Revelation is to "become" a member of one of the seven churches of
Asia to whom the book is primarily written. Stand as a worshiper in the
service. Listen to the reading of John's "letter."

When this is done, the foundation on which to interpret this
chapter is clear: **the woman that you saw is the great city which has
dominion over the kings of the earth** (v. 18). There would be no question in the minds of the members of the seven churches but that this
city, **the Great Prostitute,** was Rome.

This interpretation is supported by the fact that **the woman is
seated on seven hills** (v. 9). In the ancient world, Rome was commonly
understood to be built on seven hills. She is **drunk with the blood of the
saints and the blood of the martyrs of Jesus** (v. 6). Surely Antipas of
Pergamum was among them (2:13). **The waters where the harlot is
seated** (v. 1) symbolize **the peoples and multitudes and nations and
tongues** (v. 15) over whom Rome rules. Further, her name is **Babylon
the great,** i.e., Rome, **mother of harlots and of earth's abomination**
(v. 5).

Note that the Great Harlot is **sitting on a scarlet** Monster which
has **seven heads and ten horns** (v. 3)—surely the Vicious Monster of
13:1, i.e., the Roman Empire.

Rome's portrayal as a woman may be likened to Israel's portrayal
as a woman in the Old Testament. As Israel "played the harlot" by going after other gods and worshiping idols so Rome plays the harlot by
worshiping the emperor and the goddess Roma, the personification of
Rome, rather than the true God, the God of the seven churches of Asia.
By joining in this false worship of the emperor and the state, **the kings
of the earth** and their subjects commit **fornication** with her.

Sometimes John's characters have a fluidity to them that does not stay strictly within the rigid confines of logic. For example, the Vicious Monster has **seven heads** which are said to be both **seven hills** and **seven kings** (vv. 9-10). Again the Vicious Monster itself apparently at one time represents the empire—it has **seven heads,** i.e., **seven kings** or emperors—and at another time represents one of those kings: the Monster belongs to the seven . . . (v. 11).

The Vicious Monster is also described in words, used earlier to describe God (1:4), **who was and is not and is to come** (v. 8). This may well refer to the belief that arose after the suicide of Nero that he would rise from the dead and return at the head of an army to re-take his throne and rule over the empire (cf. v. 16). This fake messiah is the counterpart of the true Messiah, i.e., the Lamb of God, who died and was resurrected and will come again.

Verse 14 points ahead to the great battle between the Vicious Monster and his cohorts (19:11f) and **The Word of God** (19:13) who is also named **King of kings and Lord of lords** (20:16, 17:14). Be of good cheer, members of the seven churches! The Lamb will conquer them!

The identity of the kings or emperors of 17:9-12 is much disputed and is not germane to the message of the chapter. It is worth mentioning that the Roman poet Juvenal and others at the end of the first century considered the emperor Domitian to be Nero "all over again." In the vocabulary of Revelation, this would be stated, "He (Nero) was, is not (He committed suicide), and is to come (Domitian—'Nero all over again')."

Message

John envisioned the Great Prostitute, Rome, as drunk with the blood of saints and martyrs. In the aftermath of Watergate the old adage, "Power corrupts; absolute power corrupts absolutely," is still worth repeating. Humans become drunk with power. Presidents, cut off from the people and in close contact only with those who depend upon them for their own positions, can develop an exaggerated sense of their own importance and arrogate to themselves power that belongs to the people. They can use people to their own ends. They can flaunt the legal system and attempt to become a law to themselves.

Evil carries within it the seeds of its own destruction. A den of thieves makes for a very uneasy alliance. Sooner or later "the ten horns will hate the Great Prostitute, make her desolate and naked, devour her flesh, and burn her up with fire."

Rome lived in constant fear that her subject peoples would revolt and destroy her. In the end they did. Gibbon's *Rise and Fall of the Roman*

Empire tells this story. In the meantime Rome crushed rebellions with a heavy hand.

Side by side with the working out of this law of the harvest, is the dominant theme of Revelation that the Lamb will conquer the forces of evil. It is the faith of Christians as well as of John that in the final outcome God will be victorious over evil!

The United States is the chief supplier of arms to many governments. In more occasions than we like to think, those very arms are used by dictators to suppress popular movements of their own people. Too often in our attempt to prop up dictatorships in Latin America and elsewhere, we have lost the people. They have turned against us.

FALLEN, FALLEN IS BABYLON THE GREAT! 18:1-24

Introduction

This funeral dirge on "Babylon" proclaims her former greatness in order to show dramatically how far she has fallen.

A tremendous angel, so great that **the whole earth was made bright with his splendor,** comes down from heaven to exult over the doom of "Babylon" (18:1). He takes as his theme the proclamation which the second flying angel shouted to the corners of the earth, "Fallen, fallen is Babylon the great!" (14:8)

The chapter includes:

1. A description of the desolate depths to which "Babylon" has fallen

2. An invitation to God's people to **come out of her**

3. Descriptions of her unparalleled former greatness

4. Mourning for her by kings, merchants, and shipmasters

5. The reason for her demise: **In her was found the blood of prophets and of saints . . .** (v. 24)

Into Rome as capital of the empire streamed wealth, luxury, food, and even slaves from every part of the civilized world of that day. The wealth of the merchants and shippers of the world was built on the Roman peace, roads, law, and trade.

A most effective way to approach the eighteenth chapter is to read it aloud as a funeral dirge.

The Vision 18:1-24
YOU ARE THERE!
Look!   Another angel having great authority is coming   18:1

down from heaven!
His splendor lights up the whole world.
With a mighty voice he shouts: 2

Listen! *Fallen! Fallen is Babylon the Great!*
She has become the home of demons
the haunt of every unclean spirit,
the haunt of every polluted and hateful bird; for   3
she made all nations drunk with the wine of her
impure passion.
The kings of the earth have committed adultery with
her.
The businessmen of the earth have grown
rich from catering to her unrestrained lust.

Listen! Another voice from heaven calls,   4
Come out of her, O my people, lest you par-
ticipate in her sins and share in her punishment.
For her sins are piled high as heaven   5
and God remembered her crimes.
Pay her back in her own coin (give it to her in the same   6
way she gave it to you). No, more, repay her
double for what she has done.
Give her a double dose of her own medicine!
Give her as much torment and grief as the high   7
and mighty airs she gave herself when she
played the harlot.
She boasts in her heart, "I sit enthroned as a queen.
No widow, I.
In mourning I shall never be"
In one day her plagues shall strike — epidemics, be-   8
reavement, famine, and burning;
for mighty is the Lord God who has judged her
guilty.

Look! The kings of the earth who wallowed with her in in-   9
dulgence and fornication weep and wail over
her; they see the smoke from her burning.
They stand far off afraid of her torment.   10
Listen to them say,
Alas! Alas, thou great city, thou mighty city,
Babylon!
In one hour thy punishment has come.
Listen! The businessmen of the world weep and mourn for   11
her!
Look! No one buys their goods any more:
imported cargo of gold, silver, jewels and pearls,   12

fine linen, purple, silk, and scarlet, scented
wood of every kind, carvings from costly
woods, ivory, iron, and marble, cargo of cin-   13
namon, spice, incense, myrrh and frank-
incense, of wine, oil, fine flour and wheat, of
cattle and sheep, horses and chariots, and
slaves, that is, human souls.

Listen to the mighty angel!

All that you ever wanted, your heart's desires, have   14
been taken from you. All your luxury and splen-
dor has vanished never to return.

Look!   All the dealers in these goods, who became rich   15
            from her are standing afar off afraid of her pain,
            weeping and wailing,

Listen! *Alas! Alas, for the great city once bedecked as a*   16
            queen in fine linen, purple and scarlet covered
            with gold, with jewels, and with pearls!
            In one hour all your riches have been stripped   17
            from you.

Look!   All ship captains and travelers, sailors and all over-
            seas shippers stand far off and cry out when   18
            they see the sky darkened by her burning,

Listen! *What city was like the great city?*

Look!   They throw dust on their heads; they weep and   19
            mourn and cry out,

Listen! *Alas! Alas, for the great city! All ship owners grew*
            rich by her wealth. In one hour she has been
            destroyed.

            Rejoice over her, O heaven, saints, apostles, and   20
            prophets! God has taken vengeance on her! for
            what she did to you.

Look!   A mighty angel takes up a huge millstone and hurls   21
            it into the sea and says,

Listen! *So shall Babylon the Great be thrown down violently*
            and wiped out forever!
            The sound of harpists and musicians, minstrels,   22
            of flutists and trumpeters,
            shall be heard in you no more.
            Craftsmen of any kind
            shall be found in you no more.
            The sound of the millstone

> *shall be heard in you no more.*
> *The light of a lamp,*   23
> *shall shine in you no more.*
> *The voice of a bridegroom and his bride*
> *shall be heard in you no more.*
> *Your businessmen were the giants of world*
> *industry.*
> *No more!*
> *All nations were deceived by your dirty tricks.*
> *No more!*
> For in you was found the blood of God's people,   24
> *prophets, saints, and all those you killed in the*
> *world.*

Interpretation: What does the text say?

The key to understanding chapter 18 lies in the first and last verses. The first states the theme of the passage. **Fallen, fallen is "Babylon" the Great!** The last states the cause of her downfall. **In her was found the blood of prophets and saints.** To members of the seven churches of Asia, who are facing persecution and possible martyrdom, here is a cause for rejoicing for God has vindicated them. Wicked "Babylon," i.e., Rome, will meet her just reward (v. 20).

The function of the passage is not just to reassure the saints about the justice of God and give them courage, but also to summon God's people to leave the city **lest you take part in her sins, lest you share in her plagues.**

Two moods characterize this vision. The first is the exultation of the righteous people of God for the salvation wrought by God. The second is the anguish and lament of wicked earth-dwellers who have been seduced by the Great Harlot, "Babylon," i.e., Rome. With her they are now the recipients of his judgments.

Rome's plagues: **pestilence, mourning, famine,** and **fire** are to come in a single day (v. 8). The symbolism of harlotry is carried over from chapter 17:1f. **She shall be burned with fire** as were harlots from priestly families (Leviticus 21:9). In preparation for this she is to be stripped of her finery (18:16-17) and made **desolate and naked** (17:16).

Babylon, i.e., Rome, has been the hub of the civilized world. The entire empire has been dependent on her. **The kings of the earth will weep and wail when they** see the smoke of her burning (v. 9) for they know that their political power will crumble with her downfall. **The merchants of the earth will weep and mourn since no one buys their cargo any more** (v. 11). Economic catastrophe has come. The affluence of the rich has been wiped out (18:15-16). Shippers can find no one to buy their cargo (v. 19).

The fall of "Babylon," which at times (cf. v. 1) is described as already accomplished, in other places (cf. vv. 21-23) is contemplated as still to come. A member of the church at Ephesus would understand the dilemma somewhat like this: "Yes, the downfall of Rome has not happened yet, but in the will of God it has already occurred! In this sure knowledge I will have the courage to face opposition, persecution and even martyrdom!"

The picture at the end of chapter 18 is one of desolation and even death—no more harpers, minstrels, flute players, trumpeters, craftsmen, lamp shining, bridegrooms or brides. The proclamation of God's mighty angel (v. 1) is in essence repeated here. The mighty angel takes up a huge millstone and throws it into the sea (vv. 21f).

Message

John pictures the Great Harlot, Babylon, Rome, as having outward opulence but interior rottenness. This is frequently the case with evil. Evil is often arrayed in scarlet and purple, bedecked with gold, pearls, and fine jewels. She is frequently surrounded by **all articles of costly wood, bronze, iron, and marble** and in collusion with merchants, legislators and the great people of the earth.

But inwardly there is rottenness, corruption, bribery of senators and congressmen. Though outwardly a queen, inwardly she is a widow. To change the figure, evil is like a house of cards. It cannot stand. It must inevitably fall. One day a congressman, the next, disgraced and driven from office.

Come out of her, my people, lest you take part in her sins, lest you share in her plagues. . . . John knows that intercourse with evil tends to corrupt the good. Corruption of the unwary, even of the innocent, is inherent in the deceptive schemes of evil persons. The person who drives the car is as guilty as the one who robs the bank.

11
The Victory Celebration in Heaven
19:1—20:15

Introduction

The dirge is finished. "Babylon" is fallen. But victory is not complete until it is celebrated. The celebration of victory over the Great Prostitute takes place in the throne room in heaven. God is on the throne. He is surrounded by the Four Living Creatures, the Twenty-four Elders, and a great multitude (of the redeemed and of angels). They shout, "Hallelujah!" because God has judged the Great Prostitute and avenged on her the blood of his slaves.

The marriage of the Lamb and the marriage supper are announced. The bride is ready. Those who are invited to the marriage feast are blessed. The marriage supper itself is not described but is inevitably in stark contrast to the Great Supper of God of verses 17-21.

The Vision   19:1-10
YOU ARE THERE!

See!	A great multitude in heaven!	19:1
Listen!	They are shouting,	
	Hallelujah! Salvation and glory and power belong to our God!	
	His judgments are true and righteous.	2
	He has passed judgment on the Great Prostitute who corrupted the world with her fornication. He has avenged on her the blood of his slaves.	
Listen!	They are shouting once again.	3
	Hallelujah! The smoke from her burning goes up forever and ever.	
Look!	The Twenty-four Elders and the Four Living Creatures are falling down and worshiping	4

	God seated on his throne.	
Listen!	They cry, **Hallelujah!**	
Listen!	From the throne comes a voice crying,	5
	Praise our God, all you his slaves, you who hear him small and great!	

Listen to the great multitude

	Its voice sounds like the sound of many waters	6
	and mighty thunderpeals.	
Listen!	The multitude shouts	
	Hallelujah! For the Lord God the Almighty reigns!	
	Rejoice, exult, give him the glory!	7
	The marriage of the Lamb has come	
	and his Bride has put on her wedding gown.	
See!	Her gown is made of fine linen, pure white!	8
	The fine linen is the righteous deeds of Christ's slaves.	
Listen!	The interpreting angel says to John,	9
	Write this: Blessed are those who are invited to the marriage supper of the Lamb.	
Note this!	*These are the true words of God.*	
Look!	John falls at the feet of the angel to worship him, but the angel says,	10
Listen!	*You must not do that. I am a fellow slave with you and your brethren who believe the witness Jesus made by his martyrdom. This is the spirit that inspires the Christian prophet. Don't worship me. Worship God.*	

Interpretation: What does the text say?

The climax of the celebration is in verse 6 where the great multitude shouts, "Hallelujah! For the Lord our God the Almighty reigns." In a profound sense the situation here at the end in chapter 19 is the same as it was in the beginning of chapter 4. **God the Almighty reigns.** There God was on the throne, he was and is and is to come (4:8-9); here he is seated on the throne (19:4), he was and is and has come, he reigns (19:6). Both here and there the **Four Living Creatures** and the **Twenty-four Elders** fall down and worship God. The climax thus is not the vengeance on **The Great Prostitute,** Rome, but the worship of God, i.e., the ascribing of worth to God.

The threads of the tapestry of the Apocalypse are being woven together into a triumphant masterpiece. The occasion for the celebration is that the plan of God has been brought to fulfillment. **The salvation and the power and the kingdom of our God** was declared in chapter 12. The Devil, Satan, (the Great Red Dragon) was defeated in heaven by **Michael and his angels** and thrown down to earth. Now this salvation is proclaimed by the great multitude in heaven. "Thy Kingdom come on earth," the prayer of the saints, is in the process of being realized.

The passage is a fulfillment of many themes woven throughout the fabric of the book. The cry of the martyr-saints under the altar (6:10), **"How long before thou wilt judge and vindicate our blood** on the earth-dwellers?" has been fulfilled in chapter 18 by the judgment on the Great Prostitute and acknowledged in the hymn of victory here (19:2-3). The scene is a repetition of the celebration of the seventh trumpet but at a more developed stage. There (11:15-18) judgment was beginning; here (19:1f) it is in the final stages.

Who is the great multitude that shouts **Hallelujah** (literally, "Praise God")? It includes his slaves (v. 5), i.e., those who belong to God, **those who fear him small and great** (v. 5), the saints, i.e., faithful Christians, and above all the martyrs, whose **blood** has been shed (v. 2).

As part of this climactic celebration a new cause for rejoicing has been added: **the marriage of the Lamb** (v. 7) and with it the **marriage supper** (v. 9). The Lamb of course is Jesus Christ. **The Bride** symbolizes the Church for she is clothed in **fine linen, the righteous deeds** of Christians, especially the martyrs (vv. 8-9). She also symbolizes the **New Jerusalem** (21:2). **Her fine linen bright and pure** (19:8) is in striking contrast to the dress of the Great Prostitute (17:4).

The marriage supper of the Lamb (19:9) could only be understood by members in the seven churches as the Lord's Supper to be celebrated anew in the Kingdom of God (cf. Mark 14:25; Luke 22:16).

The testimony of Jesus is the Spirit of prophecy (19:10) probably means that the witness that Jesus made by his death is the spirit that inspires the prophets. To this witness both John and the interpreting angel hold fast (vv. 9-10).

The celebration in this chapter is anticipatory. Great "battles" against the Vicious Monster, the False Prophet, and the Great Red Dragon have yet to be fought. Victory is certain. In that sense it has already occurred but it is also coming in 19:11 — 20:15.

THE GREAT SUPPER OF GOD   19:11-21

Introduction

Time and eternity, present and future, are intertwined throughout the book of Revelation. But at the same time there is movement toward the end. This involves an intensification of the action.

Now we come to one of the last events: the final victory over the Vicious Monster and the False Prophet. The battle lines are drawn. On the one side the Word of God and the armies of heaven, on the other, the kings of the earth and their armies under the leadership of the Vicious Monster and the False Prophet. The Word of God is victorious. The Monster and the False Prophet are thrown into the lake of fire that burns with brimstone. The earth-dwellers are slain by the sword from the mouth of the Messiah and all the birds are gorged with their flesh.

The Vision 19:11-21
YOU ARE THERE!

Look!	Heaven opens! Lo! A white horse!	19:11
Look!	The rider is called Faithful and True; he makes war and judges rightly.	
Look!	His eyes are like blazing fire. Many crowns grace his head. His name is known only to himself.	12
	His robe drips blood. He is called the Word of God.	13
Look!	A sharp sword comes from his mouth; an iron rod is in his hand. The sword is to smite nations; the rod to rule them.	15
Note this!	He will tread the wine press of the fury of the wrath of God Almighty.	
Look!	On his robe and his thigh is written, *King of Kings and Lord of Lords.*	16
See!	The armies of heaven clothed in pure white linen and mounted on white horses follow him.	14
Look!	A mighty angel standing in the sun, shouts to all the birds flying in heaven,	17
Listen!	*Come, gather for God's great supper: to eat the flesh of kings, the flesh of commanders, the flesh of men of valor, the flesh of horses and riders, the flesh of all men, free and slaves, peasants and nobles.*	18

Look!	The Vicious Monster and the kings of the world have gathered their armies to make war against The Word of God!	19
See!	The Monster and the False Prophet are taken captive.	20
Look!	The two are thrown alive into the fiery lake that burns with brimstone.	
	The rest of the world's armies are slaughtered by the sword issuing from the mouth of the Word of God.	21
See!	All the birds are gorged with their flesh.	

Interpretation: What does the text say!

The identity of the leader of the armies of heaven is clear. He is described as having **a sharp sword** issuing **from his mouth** as did the risen Christ of 1:16. He is to rule the nations **with a rod of iron** as was the destiny of the male child who was snatched up to God's throne in 12:5. As in 3:14 he is called **Faithful and True.** His name inscribed **on his robe and thigh** is **King of Kings and Lord of Lords.** He is clearly the Messiah.

Opposing him are the vicious Monster and the False Prophet (cf. 13) together with the **kings of the earth.** These are the political and religious leaders and the vassal kings of the Roman Empire.

Only the outcome of the battle is described. The Vicious Monster and the False Prophet are defeated and **thrown alive into the lake of fire that burns with brimstone** (v. 20). Their followers, the earth-dwellers, were **slain by the sword of him who sits upon the** white **horse,** i.e., the Messiah. They provide the menu for **the great supper of God** (vv. 17-21). The Messiah wins the battle not by physical force but by **the Word of God.** This is the **sharp sword** which **issues from his mouth.** In the Bible God's Word is living and active (Hebrews 4:12) and is intimately connected with his acts. In Genesis God says, "Let there be light." And there was light. The Word of God is the Gospel, the good news that God has acted in Jesus Christ for the salvation of men. His weapons include righteousness or justice with which he judges (v. 11) and are characterized by faithfulness (v. 11) to his covenant word.

In stark contrast to the Messiah's weapons are those of the Monster and the False Prophet. Their arsenal is deceit, falsehood, and fake miracles. With these they gather the kings of the earth and deceive the earth-dwellers.

The **armies of heaven** have no weapons but their garments **of fine** linen, white and pure (v. 14), i.e., their **righteous deeds** (v. 8). They are the conquerors who have been given white garments (cf. 3:5). In 6:11 the martyrs are each given a white robe. There is no indication here that the saints have any part in the battle other than accompanying the Messiah. It is his victory won by the sword issuing from his mouth.

Message

Hallelujah! Salvation and glory and power belong to our God! The exaltation of victory leads to exultation and paeans of praise. The rehearsal of the greatness of the character and deeds of God is a powerful hormone for the strengthening of faith. The Christian affirms that God is able, that he has brought salvation, that the Almighty reigns! Out of the certainty of faith, John depicts the finality of the conquest of the forces of evil that confront the church. Christ is **Faithful and True**; he is **The Word of God,** sharper than a two-edged sword; he is **King of Kings and Lord of Lords.** Because he is all these, he is able to conquer every foe. This is the faith of the Christian. This is the faith that gives the Christian the power to keep going on.

THE FINAL TRIUMPH   20:1-15

Introduction

The final defeat of the Vicious Monster and the False Prophet leaves only the demonic archenemy, Satan, the Great Red Dragon, to be overcome. Then the faithful will be rewarded and God's kingdom will come on earth.

The section is made up of four events.
1. The Binding of Satan (20:1-3)
2. The Reign of Martyrs With Christ (vv. 4-6)
3. The Final Victory Over Satan (vv. 7-10)
4. The Final Judgment (vv. 11-15)

The twentieth chapter has definite affinities with the events of chapters 12 and 13 where Satan is thrown down from heaven to earth and Christians are martyred for not worshiping the Monster. Here he is thrown down from earth into the abyss.

An angel comes down to earth where Satan has been persecuting the Christians. He binds the Great Red Dragon with an enormous chain and throws him into the abyss, and locks the door.

The martyrs come to life and reign with Christ for a "thousand years."

(In preparation for envisioning the events of chapter 20, go back and see again the size of Satan, the Great Red Dragon in 12:1-4).

The Vision 20:1-6
YOU ARE THERE!

Look!	An angel is coming down from heaven carrying a great chain and a key in his hand.	20:1
	He seizes the Dragon, the ancient snake who is called the Devil and Satan,	2
	binds him in chains and hurls him into the bottomless pit for a thousand years, locks it and seals it so that he cannot deceive the nations until the thousand years are over.	3
	Afterwards he must be released for a little while.	
Look!	Sitting on thrones as judges are the souls of the martyrs, beheaded for their loyal testimony to Jesus and the saving purpose of God.	4
	They have not worshiped the Monster or its statue nor received its brand on their foreheads or hands.	
	They come to life and reign as priests of God with Christ for a thousand years.	
Note this!	Blessed and holy are those who participate in the first resurrection! Over them the second death has no power.	6

Interpretation: What does the text say?

1. The Binding of Satan (vv. 1-3)

The angel, God's emissary, in verse 1 comes from heaven, where the Great Red Dragon was, to earth where the Dragon now is, seizes him, binds him with a huge chain, and hurls him into the bottomless pit, shuts it, locks it, and seals it. Conceivably this angel could be Michael who defeated the Dragon and was instrumental in throwing him out of heaven down to earth in 12:7-9.

In 19:11-21 the earthly human representatives of the Great Red Dragon, namely the Vicious Monster and the False Prophet were finally overcome. But the Devil, the demonic spiritual force behind the human, remained to be vanquished decisively.

The demonic power of the Devil is so strong that even when he was bound with a huge chain, hurled into the abyss, locked in, and the door was **sealed,** he still after the thousand years **must be loosed for a little**

while (v. 3). Sealing implies that Satan could not break the seal himself.

The fundamental sin of Satan is the deception of men and women (v. 3). He attempts to usurp the place of God and get men to worship him rather than the Creator.

2. The Reign of the Martyrs With Christ (vv. 4-6)

Who are those who **reign with Christ** for **a thousand years?** Verse 4 does not specifically identify them. However, the rest of the verse does. They are **those who had been beheaded for** their **witness to Jesus Christ** and for carrying out God's saving purpose. They are the martyrs, **who had not worshiped** the Monster (the Roman emperor) and **had not received his brand on their foreheads or their hands** (v. 4). The cry of the martyrs (6:9-11) for justice has been answered. No longer are they under the altar; they are reigning with Christ.

Controversy over the significance of the thousand-year reign has caused a great harm to the church. Much attention has been given to speculation and debate about this subject. Yet these seven verses are the only verses in the entire Bible of 66 books, 1,189 chapters, and 31,173 verses where the thousand-year reign is mentioned.

How are we to understand the thousand-year reign? What is its meaning here? In Revelation it is probably to be understood as a special reward for the martyrs. At most the group might include the confessors, those who confessed faith in Jesus but did not worship the Monster or its image (v. 4).

Since numbers in Revelation are symbolic, the thousand years should not be taken literally but at most as "a considerable length of time." Other apocalypses, both Christian and Jewish, have similar lengths of time varying from forty to seven thousand years. It may be helpful to remember that 2 Peter 2:8 says, " . . . with the Lord one day is as a thousand years and a thousand years as a day." This certainly cautions us against literalizing a thousand years in Revelation.

Special Note. Certain Old Testament prophets who lived before the idea of resurrection had arisen in Israel looked forward to a time in the future within history on earth when the golden age of God's kingdom would come into reality. (Cf. Amos 9:13-15; Micah 4:1-7). Belief in the resurrection and the concept of the future life in heaven arose later, in the time period between the Old and New Testaments. Jerusalem had fallen; Judah was taken captive to Babylon. Many lost hope of reestablishing the kingdom on earth. For some, future hope now became the hope of resurrection and a life in heaven. The older prophetic hope of setting up the kingdom again in Judah and Israel with Jerusalem as capitol becomes compressed in some apocalyptic writings into a kind of "millenium" of various lengths, a temporary kingdom on earth before the final consummation of all things. In Revelation the old earth passes away; a *new* heaven and a *new* earth replace the old. The thousand-year temporary reign on earth for John probably originated in the older prophetic hope for the restoration of the earthly kingdom in history and functions in John's writing as a special reward for the martyrs.

The Vision of the Victory Over Satan   20:7-10
YOU ARE THERE!

Note!	The thousand years are at an end.	20:7
Look!	Satan is untied and released from the bottomless pit.	
	He goes forth to the four corners of the earth to deceive the nations, Gog and Magog, to muster them for battle.	8
Look!	The warriors are like the sand of the sea in number.	
	They march to the broad plain; they lay siege to the beloved city and to the camp of God's people.	9
Look!	Fire comes down from heaven and devours them!	
	The Devil, their deceiver, is taken up and hurled into the lake of fire and sulphur where the Monster and the False Prophet are.	10
	They are tortured day and night forever and ever.	

The Vision of the Last Judgment   20:11-15
YOU ARE THERE!

Look!	Earth and sky flee in terror from him who is sitting on the great white throne. They cannot be found.	20:11
	The dead come up out of the sea. Death and Hades give up the dead in them.	13
	All the dead, great and small, stand before the throne.	12

> The record books are opened;
> another book, the Book of Life is opened.
> The dead are judged by what is written in
> the record books, by what they have done.
> Then Death and Hades are taken up and hurled   14
> into the lake of fire and sulphur.

Hear this!   This is the second death; if anyone's name is not   15
found written in the Book of Life he is
thrown into the lake of fire and sulphur.

Interpretation: What does the text say?

3. The Final Victory Over Satan (vv. 7-10)

The Monster and the False Prophet, the persecutors of the church, were decisively defeated in chapter 19. All that remains for the victory to be final is for Satan, the spiritual power behind the Monster and the False Prophet, to be destroyed. This is pictured in the context of a great final battle in which the great deceiver, the Devil, and the armies of the nations surround **the camp of the saints and the beloved city. Gog and Magog** represent the enemies of the people of God, the true Christians. Fire from heaven, i.e., from God, consumes them. The Devil is **thrown into the lake of fire and brimstone to be tormented day and night for ever and ever** (v. 10). The gigantic struggle between good and evil is over. The Messiah had conquered the enemies of his church on earth (19:11-21). God then disposed of his archenemy in the spiritual realm, the Devil (20:7-10). All that is yet to come is the last judgment with the rewards and punishments related to it.

4. The Last Judgment (vv. 11-15)

In this picture of the last judgment all are brought before God's judgment throne. They are judged according to their deeds. Presumably the martyrs would not be in this company for they have received their reward already.

The last enemies of mankind are disposed of. Death and Hades are **thrown into the lake of fire.** This is highly symbolic language. John is using pictures again to express eternal truth. What it means is that the victory over evil is complete and final.

Message

The final defeat of the Devil and the last judgment dominate chapter 20. There is a personal character to evil that is known in the Bible as Satan or the Devil. It is with men and women that Satan has to do. It is they whom he corrupts. Evil is not only personal; it is also transpersonal. It is pictured in the scriptures as coming into human life from outside. Consequently the Devil is portrayed as demonic. It is this aspect of evil that is related to the structures of society that force some people to live in ghettos and that dehumanize persons in mass industries.

But this fact does not excuse persons from the responsibility for their own actions. In the scene of the last judgment this is abundantly made clear. All are judged "by what they had done." The viewpoint of John is that with the last judgment, punishment is final; the oportunity for repentance has passed. Those whose works have been evil, i.e., whose names are not written in the book of life, are "thrown into the lake of fire and brimstone" and they will be tormented day and night for ever and ever. This symbolic language means that God cannot be toyed with forever. There comes that day of reckoning when the books will be closed and the verdict rendered. The disobedient and unrepentant will be separated from God and Christ. They will not be a part of the kingdom of God. There can be no greater judgment, there can be no severer punishment than separation and exclusion from the kingdom. The verdict is not so much rendered by God as it is chosen by persons in their refusal to repent. It is in this way that they are judged "by what they had done" (v. 12).

Those whose loyalty to Christ has been steadfast will reign with him in his kingdom.

12
The New Jerusalem
21:1—22:21

Introduction

The goal of the book of Revelation and of history is reached in the vision of the new heaven, the new earth, and the new Jerusalem. The saving purpose of God is accomplished. The dwelling of God is with his people (21:1-8). The visions following are enlargements on that theme.

Just as the fall of Babylon, announced in 16:17-21, was detailed in chapters 17 and 18, so the realization of the Kingdom of God in the new Jerusalem on earth is presented in a kind of snapshot in 21:1-8 and enlarged on in 21:9—22:5.

The Visions may be outlined as follows:
1. Vision of the New Creation (21:1-8)
2. The View of the Holy City From Outside (21:9-14)
3. The Measurement of the Walls (vv. 15-17)
4. The Description of the City (vv. 18-21)
5. The Glory of the Holy City (vv. 22-27)
6. The City as the New Eden (22:1-5)

John is whisked away in the Spirit to a very high mountain. There he sees the Bride, the wife of the Lamb, as the new Jerusalem coming down out of heaven from God.

The city has twelve gates named for the twelve tribes of Israel. It has also twelve foundations named for the twelve apostles. It is a cube 1,500 miles in length, breadth, and height. The walls are of precious stones and the gates of single pearls.

There is no temple in the city for God and the Lamb are its temple. They are also the source of light. All the glory of the nations comes into the new Jerusalem. Only the followers of the Lamb can live in it.

The Vision of the New Creation   21:1-8

These are highly symbolic visions. You will want to visualize them by asking, what does the text say?

YOU ARE THERE!

Look!	A new heaven and a new earth!	21:1
	The first heaven and the first earth are gone.	
	The sea has disappeared.	
Look!	The Holy City, the new Jerusalem, is coming down out of heaven, beautiful as a bride ready for her husband.	2
Listen!	The voice from the throne announces, *Hear this! God's home is now with people. He will live with them and they will be his people.*	3
Note this!	*He will wipe every tear from their eyes. There will be no more death, nor mourning, nor crying, nor pain. The old conditions have vanished.*	4
Listen!	He who sits on the throne says, *Hear this! I make everything new. Write it down, for these words are true and are to be trusted.*	5
Note this!	*It is done! I am the Alpha and Omega, the beginning and the end.*	6
And this!	*To the thirsty I shall give water without charge, water from the fountain of life without charge.*	
	The victors will receive this inheritance from me, I will be their God and they will be my people.	7
Hear this!	*But the cowards, the faithless, the perverts, the immoral, the sorcerers, the idolaters, and all liars will be thrown into the lake that burns with fire and brimstone. This is the second death.*	8

Interpretation: What does the text say?

It is not enough to have conquered and punished the Devil (the Great Red Dragon), and the persecutors of God's people, (the Vicious Monster, the False Prophet, and the earth-dwellers), Rome, and her allies. The saving purpose of God is not complete until his kingdom comes on earth and his people are rewarded. Only then can God finally say, "It is done!" (v. 6)

It is understandable that **a new earth** is needed in the consummation for **the first earth** had its pain, tears, and imperfections. Perhaps the very presence of Satan in heaven (12:1-8) was enough for the prophet to envision the need for **a new heaven**. Jerusalem too is not the old Jerusalem but a **new Jerusalem.**

With this the promise of the covenant of the Old and of the New Testament is fulfilled, **the dwelling of God is with man. He will dwell with them, and they shall be his people, and God himself will be with them** (v. 3).

All the sorrows of earthly existence will be wiped away; all infirmities and pain will cease, and **death shall be no more.**

For God makes everything new (v. 5). He is the creator, **the Alpha and the Omega,** i.e., **the first and the last, the beginning and the end.** It is his goodness, his mercy, his bounty, that he makes available to any who truly thirsts for salvation. It is a gift of his grace; it is without price. He gives it to the one **who conquers,** to the one who is faithful and loyal to Christ in the face of trial, persecution, and even martyrdom. **I will be his God and he shall be my son** (v. 7). He will belong to the family of God.

John is not hesitant to state the reality of God's judgment. The sins mentioned here are not meant to refer to sin in general but are those sins which arose in connection with the worship of the goddess Roma and the emperor and the situations faced by members of the seven churches in Asia. The **cowardly** are those who do not have the courage to resist the social and political pressure to worship the emperor. The **faithless** are not those who disbelieve but rather those who were not faithful in the face of trial. The **polluted** are those who have committed fornication with the Great Harlot, Rome (17:2). The **murderers** would include those who slew the martyrs (13:15). Fornication, sorcery, and idolatry are particularly connected with idol worship (cf. 9:20-21). **Liars** would refer to the followers of the great deceivers, the Devil, the Monster, and the False Prophet. No lie is found in the mouths of the martyrs (14:5). The eternal destiny of all earth-dwellers who follow the great liar is the **lake that burns with fire and brimstone** (v. 8.).

The Vision of the Holy City   21:9-27
YOU ARE THERE!

Look!   Then one of the seven angels who had the   21:9
                      seven bowls full of the seven last
                      plagues says to John,
                      Come, I will show you the Bride, the wife of

the Lamb.

Look!   In the Spirit the angel whisks John away to   10
a very high mountain.

He sees the Holy City Jerusalem coming
down out of heaven from God.

The splendor of God envelopes it; its radi-   11
ance is like a precious jewel, like jasper,
clear as crystal.

Look!   The city has a great high wall with twelve   12
gates; at the gates twelve angels.

Inscribed on the gates are the names of the
twelve tribes of the sons of Israel.

on the east three gates,   13
on the north three gates,
on the south three gates,
and on the west three gates.

Look!   The city wall rests on twelve foundations.   14
On them are written twelve names of
the twelve apostles of the Lamb.

Look!   The angel has a measuring rod of gold in his   15
hand to measure the city, its gates, and
its walls.

Note this!   The city is a perfect cube; its length,   16
breadth, and height are equal; 1,500
miles long, 1,500 miles broad, and
1,500 miles high.

And this!   The wall is 260 feet high, by a man's meas-   17
ure; that is, an angel's.

Look!   The city is of pure gold, transparent as glass.

The wall is made of jasper.   18

The foundations of the wall are faced with   19
all kinds of precious stones:

the first is jasper, the second sapphire,
the third agate, the fourth emerald, the
fifth onyx, the sixth carnelian, the   20
seventh chrysolite, the eighth beryl, the
ninth topaz, the tenth chrysoprase, the
eleventh jacinth, the twelfth amethyst.

Look!   The twelve gates of the city are each made   21
from a single pearl. The street of the
city is pure gold, transparent as glass.

Look!   The city needs no temple,   22
for its temple is the Lord God the
Almighty and the Lamb.

	The city needs no sunlight or moonlight, for the splendor of God and the Lamb floods it with light.	23
	In its light the nations walk and the kings of the earth bring all their glory and honor into it.	24 26
	The gates are never shut and there is no night there.	25
And this!	Only those whose names are written in the Lamb's book of life get in—no liars or perverts, nor anything defiled.	27

The Vision of the City as the New Eden   22:1-6
YOU ARE THERE!

Look!	The angel shows John the river of the water of life, sparkling like crystal.	22:1
	It flows from the throne of God and the Lamb down the middle of the city's street.	2
	On both sides of the river is the tree of life. It bears twelve kinds of fruit, one each month.	
Note this!	The leaves of the tree are for the healing of the nations!	
Look!	The throne of God and of the Lamb! His slaves are worshiping him.	3
	They see his face.	4
	His name is inscribed on their foreheads.	
Note this!	There is no night! No lamp! No sun! For the Lord God is the light of the city.	5
Rejoice!	His slaves reign for ever and ever.	

Interpretation: What does the text say?

This is a symbolic portrait of the idealized Jerusalem, the eternal city of God and of the redeemed. The city comes from **heaven, from God,** and differs in almost every respect from the old Jerusalem of the "first earth." There's **no temple** there for **God and the Lamb** function as **its temple.** There's **no sun** or **moon** there for the **glory of God** and the **lamp** of the **Lamb** illumines it. There's no hunger or death there for the **tree of life** bears **fruit every month** and its **leaves** bring **healing** to **the nations.** There's no thirst there for **the river** that flows through the midst of the city brings **the water of life.** There are no tears or sorrow or mourning or crying or pain for God has wiped all these away.

This vision of the eternal Holy City is composed of the finest treasures earth has to offer: pure gold, precious jewels, pearls, a throne, a sparkling river, twelve kinds of fruit, and abundant light.

But these treasures are to be understood symbolically. They are not to be taken literally. That this is true is clear when we look at the details. For example, the **street of the city** is said to be **pure gold, transparent as glass** (v. 21). Now gold is a very heavy, solid, opaque metal. In no way can it be said literally to **be transparent as glass.**

Again the city is said to be 1,500 miles in length, 1,500 miles in width, 1,500 miles in height as well as to have **twelve foundations.** It is all but impossible to take this literally. For a city wall to have twelve foundations the city would have to have been rebuilt on the same site twelve times! The new Jerusalem is built only once.

These symbolic pictures must be interpreted in terms of spiritual and moral values and interpersonal relationships and not in materialistic or spatial categories. For example, John writes that on the twelve foundations were **the twelve names of the twelve apostles of the Lamb.** In other words the foundations are not made of brick and mortar or stone. The life and work of the apostles of Jesus Christ are the foundations on which the New Jerusalem is built. Even here we need to be careful not to be too literal for certainly Judas would not be included, Matthias might be. However, the New Testament mentions other apostles also (cf. Acts 14:4; Galatians 1:19, etc.).

The View of the Holy City From Outside (21:9-14)

Note that verse 9, **one of the seven angels who had the seven bowls full of the seven last plagues,** ties this vision in with that of 17:1f. **The Bride** and the **new Jerusalem** are the direct counterparts to the Great Harlot (17:1f) and Babylon (ch. 18), who embody all of the sins listed in 21:8.

The Bride, the wife of the Lamb (v. 9), symbolically represents the new Jerusalem (vv. 2, 9-10), as well as the church, the congregation of the faithful (19:7-8). It may represent the martyrs in particular.

The chief point of this passage, however, is that the Holy City Jerusalem has the **glory of God. Glory** is the word most often used in the Bible to indicate the presence of God. The chief glory of the new Jerusalem is that God is present.

The Measurement of the City (vv. 15-17)

Here the issue is not one of protection as in 11:1f, but simply a part of the picture of the magnificence of the city.

The Description of the City (vv. 18-21)

The gates in ancient city walls included a tower. A single pearl huge enough to encompass a city gate and tower staggers the imagination. Again as with the jeweled walls and the golden street, the pearl gates add to the grand picture of the magnificence of the city.

The Glory of the Holy City (vv. 22-27)

Once more John is speaking symbolically. By definition, a temple is a place where God dwells. But there is no temple here, i.e., we are not dealing with a special phenomenon but with the presence of God. God's **glory** is sufficient **light** for all persons, nations and kings. John's vision reflects the ancient hope of the prophets that God would dwell in Jerusalem and that the knowledge of the glory of God would cover the earth. All men would walk in its light and bring all their glory and honor to God in Jerusalem. God is adequate for protection; there is no need to **shut the gates.** The gates are open so that all **the nations** may **bring** their **glory** and **honor** into God. Only the redeemed, **those who are written in the Lamb's book of life,** can live in the new city (v. 27).

The City as the New Eden (22:1-5)

The background of the imagery here is the Garden of Eden. The original innocence in the Garden has its final counterpart in the perfection of the redeemed in the Holy City. The companionship of God with Adam in the beginning finds the fulfillment of its promise in the fellowship of man with God and the Lamb in the new Eden. **His servants shall worship him; they shall see his face, and his name shall be on their foreheads . . . and they shall reign for ever and ever** (22:3-5). **Amen!**

Message

Thank God Revelation does not end with the last judgment! Thank God that it ends with the new heaven and the new earth!

With the new Jerusalem, the Holy City that comes down out of heaven!

With the new Eden where God dwells with his people! Where he wipes away every tear from their eyes. Where there is no more death. Where there is no mourning, nor crying, nor pain. Where all things have become new.

With the new Eden where the water of life flows bright as crystal from the throne of God and of the Lamb and the fruit of the tree of life is for the healing of the nations! Where man and woman achieve their true end, the worship of God and the Lamb. Where at last everyone of the redeemed shall see God face to face. Where they shall reign with him forever and forever on the new earth in the Kingdom of God! Amen!

EPILOGUE   22:6-21

Introduction

The visions are completed. What follows is epilogue. The purpose of the epilogue is to authenticate the message of the book so that those who hear the book read aloud in the worship service in the churches (1:3) will obey it (22:7).

The speaker in the epilogue varies but the message remains the same. The various speakers are: Christ's angel messenger, John, Christ himself, and the Holy Spirit.

It is not always possible in the epilogue to be certain who is speaking. However the message is clear. Focus on it.

Vision   22:6-21
YOU ARE THERE!

Listen!	The angel is speaking to John:	22:6
	These promises are reliable and true.	
	The Lord, the God of the spirits of the prophets, sent his angel-messenger to show his slaves what has to happen soon.	
Listen!	Jesus says, *I am coming soon.*	7
	Blessed is the one who obeys the inspired messages which are in this book.	
See!	John falls down to worship at the feet of the interpreting angel. But the angel says,	8 9
Listen!	*Don't do that! I am a fellow slave with you and your brothers the prophets and with those who keep the commands of this book. Worship God!*	
Listen!	The angel says to John,	10
	Don't seal up the commands of this prophecy for the time is near.	
	Let the evil doer do worse and	11

worse and the filthy become filthier, and the just, more righteous and the holy become holier.

Hear this! *I am coming soon! I am bringing my rewards and will repay everyone for what he has done!* 12

I am the Alpha and the Omega, the first and the last, the beginning and the end. 13

Listen! *Blessed are those who wash their garments that they may have the right to eat of the tree of life and enter the city by the gates.* 14

But without are the dogs who practice magic and fornications and commit murder and worship idols, and speak lies. 15

Listen! *I, Jesus, have sent my messenger to you with this witness. I am the root and offspring of David, the bright and morning star.* 16

Hear this! The Spirit and the Bride say, *Come!* 17
Let him who hears say, *Come!*
Let the one who hears and is thirsty, *Come!*
Let him who desires take the water of life freely.

Give heed! If you add to this book, God will add to you the plagues described in this book! 18

If you take away from the words of this book, God will take away your share in the tree of life and in the holy city. 19

Hear this! *I am coming soon,* says Jesus. 20
And this! *Amen, Come, Lord Jesus!*
The grace of the Lord Jesus be with all the saints. Amen! 21

Interpretation and Message: What does the text say?

The content of the epilogue is made up of a somewhat miscellaneous group of affirmations and exhortations from God, Christ, the Spirit, an interpreting angel, and John.

The function of the epilogue is essentially the same as the function of the prologue (1:1-8). It is to authenticate the message of Revelation and to get the members of the churches of Asia to keep, i.e., to obey, that message.

They face various situations: martyrdom, persecution, heresy within, the inertia of riches, poverty, lukewarmness, imprisonment (cf. chs. 2-3). Confronted by these trials they are to **keep the words of this book,** to remain steadfast under all circumstances, to be faithful unto death.

The message of the book is **trustworthy and true** (v. 6) as Christ was trustworthy and true (19:11; 3:14). It can be relied on. It will come to pass **soon** (v. 6). The Lord is coming speedily (v. 7).

If you obey the message of the book (v. 7) you will be given eternal life (v. 14) and be with God (vv. 14, 19). You will be happy (vv. 7, 14). Everyone reaps the rewards of his deeds (v. 12). Be prepared for Jesus is **coming soon** (vv. 7, 12, 20).

Don't worship angels, **worship God** (vv. 8-9).

Leave the scroll (Revelation) open so that all may read. There is practically no time to change the pattern of one's life (v. 11). Nevertheless the Spirit and the church exhort all who are thirsting for righteousness and eternal life to come and receive it freely (v. 17).

Those who do not heed the message of this book will not have eternal life with God but will reap the judgment of their own deeds (vv. 11, 15, 19).

As George Ladd well says[1] verses 18 and 19 are not intended to teach theology nor a mechanical theory of the inspiration of the Bible. Instead John wants the reader to take to heart the message of Revelation and act on it in his own life. For everyone will be repaid according to what he has done (v. 12). John feels so strongly about this that he says, if you don't incorporate the truth of my message into your living you will not have eternal life.

---

1. Ladd, George E., *Commentary on the Revelation of John.* Eerdman, 1971, pp. 295-296.

13
A Theology of the Book of Revelation

The context for understanding the theology of Revelation is as follows: John sees the dominant threat to the churches of Asia Minor as the demand of the Roman Empire for absolute loyalty and the worship of the emperors, living and dead, as gods and of Roma, the personification of Rome as a goddess. He sees the sword as martyrdom hanging over the head of the church like the sword of Damocles, suspended by a thread. The great temptation was compromise; the enemy from without was reinforced by the enemy from within! Compromise!—Participation in pagan feasts and festivals, worship of Roma and of the emperor, following the false "Christian" prophets, faithlessness, preoccupation with luxury and wealth, lack of love, lukewarm religion, and even immorality. This was the situation as seen through John's eyes.

John had a pastor's heart. He had a deep love for his people and a deep love for God. He longed for his people to be enthusiastic and faithful to God as he had come to know him in Jesus Christ. He earnestly desired that they would experience the reality of the presence of the risen, glorified Christ in the worshiping community of faith. He wanted them to let that experience be the undergirding foundation which would enable them to withstand the eroding acids of complacency and controversy within the churches and the compelling pressures of social, economic, and political conformity from without. He wanted desperately to strengthen their faith to withstand incipient and impending persecution, to face martyrdom with what he calls, "unflinching loyalty."

So John wrote Revelation and sent it to the seven churches of Asia. It was his witness to the saving action of God. In a deep sense it was his confession of faith. It was an attempt to communicate his faith to his Christian brothers and sisters through words and visions and thereby strengthen their faith.

The foundation upon which John's life and the entire book of Revelation is built is the sovereignty of God. God is referred to almost three times as frequently as Jesus and almost six times as often as the Devil.

John's understanding of God is best seen against the background of his cosmology. The framework within which John thinks is that of a three-storied universe: heaven, earth, and under-the-earth. Heaven is the temporary abode of God, Christ, and the angels. Earth, the temporary dwelling place of humanity, is for the present under the control of Satan and his allies. It is the battleground for the fierce struggle for the souls of men and women between the forces of good and evil. Under-the-earth consists of Hades, which is the temporary home of most of the dead, the Abyss where disobedient spirits are imprisoned, and the Lake of Fire and Brimstone.

At the apex of the universe, God is enthroned in his throne room in heaven. He is surrounded by his court consisting of the Four Living Creatures, the Seven Spirits of God, the Twenty-four Elders, the Lamb, and innumerable hosts of angels.

Thus the dominating image of Revelation depicts God as the Enthroned One. He is absolute sovereign. All things are under his control. By his will he created all things and by his will they exist. God is eternal and yet he is also the Coming One. He "was and is to come." He is Almighty. As the Enthroned One, he is also the Ruler and Re-creator. As Re-creator he makes all things new. As the Coming One he consummates history, dwells with us, wipes away every tear, and gives the water of life freely. He is our God and we are his people. We will dwell in the New Jerusalem, the New Heaven and the New Earth, the New Eden. Truly he is "the Beginning and the End."

John views the relation between heaven and earth in several ways. Heaven is the place where Michael and the angels of God fight the decisive battle with Satan and his demons (12:7-12). This heavenly drama predetermines the victory that is to occur on earth (12:12-13).

John sees the Lamb as the essential link between heaven and earth. While angels perform important functions as messengers of God, in the last analysis the Lamb is the decisive mediator of judgment and of salvation. Through him, God, dwelling in the throne room in heaven, works wrath on the Devil, the Monster, and the False Prophet. On earth, the Lamb accomplishes his redemptive work through his death. As "the Word of God" he defeats the Monster and the False Prophet.

Thus most of the action in Revelation is initiated and directed from heaven but is carried out on earth. The effects are felt throughout the universe. The Lamb opens each of the seven seals before the throne in heaven but the plagues fall on the unrepentant on earth. In similar fashion the seven bowls of the wrath of God are poured onto the earth. It is only in the consummation that the New Jerusalem comes down from heaven and that God dwells on earth (the New Earth) with men and women in the New Eden.

The character of God as "the wholly Other" may be seen in the ways in which God and his actions are portrayed indirectly. While God is the ultimate source of John's revelation, Jesus Christ is the mediating source. In fact the revelation comes to John through mediation of angels (1:1, etc.) rather than directly by God himself. It is the Lamb not God who opens the scroll; it is the Four Living Creatures who command the four horsemen of the Apocalypse to "Come!" Again and again angels carry the commands and act for God with absolute authority and power. Occasionally the temple replaces angels. Even when God himself is represented as speaking, circumlocution is still evident, " . . . he who sat upon the throne said . . . "

The purpose of portraying God as "the wholly Other" is to point to the uniqueness of God and to acknowledge the mystery that surrounds his person. He is too great for the mind of humans to comprehend. Because he alone is creator, almighty, and holy, he is worthy of worship.

The reality of his presence and of his overwhelming greatness is experienced as the community worships. Worshipers in the seven churches in Asia join with the heavenly hosts in singing, "Holy, holy, holy, is the Lord God Almighty . . . To him be blessing and honor and glory and might for ever and ever!" The Christian worships a "distant" God who also comes near. This is a miracle almost too stupendous to comprehend, almost too tremendous to believe!

In view of the foundational character of God for John's theology it is amazing that the unique terminology used for God is so limited. He is "King of the Ages." He is creator of heaven, the earth, and the sea. He has angels. He is "the One who is, who was, and who is coming."

Most of the other terms for and about God are also used regarding Jesus. He too is "Lord." The wrath is the wrath of God and the Lamb. He too is the Alpha and Omega, the Beginning and the End. He too reigns for ever and ever. He too is the temple and the light and occupies the throne of the New Jerusalem. The water of life comes from the throne he occupies together with God. He too is worthy of and receives

worship. He too is judge and savior. These designations clearly place
Jesus in a special relationship to God; in fact they place him in the
category of deity—Jesus, too, is God.

In light of the fact that God is so clearly the foundation for John's
theology yet so few unique statements are made about him, it is amazing
to note the abundance and fullness of the terms used for Jesus Christ. He
is Lord of lords and King of kings. He is Son of Man and Son of God. He
is the Faithful Martyr. He is the Word of God. He is the Root and Offspring of David, the Bright and Morning Star, and the Firstborn of the
Dead. He is Faithful and True. He rules with a rod of iron, and treads
the winepress of God's wrath. He is the shepherd who guides the faithful
to springs of living water. He has twelve apostles and is the leader of the
144,000 redeemed.

The reason for this fullness no doubt is that for John, Jesus is "the
near side of God." Jesus is therefore indispensable to his faith. God the
Almighty dwells in the throne room in heaven. Jesus Christ is present on
earth: first, as the One who was crucified, and now, as the Resurrected
Son of Man who is in the midst of the churches. He is the mediator of
God and of salvation to man. In him we see what God is like. In his life,
death, and resurrection we discover God's saving purpose. We find the
God who is coming (1:4) in the one who has come (5:9) and who is com-
ing soon (22:20).

In the initial vision of Revelation, the glorified Christ so knocks
John off of his feet that he becomes as one dead. It is a vision of Christ as
the resurrected Christ in high priestly and regal glory. The vision is that
of a divine figure in the midst of the churches of Asia holding the angels
of the churches in his right hand. As mediator of life and death, he has
the ultimate power over Death and Hades. The two-edged sword of the
Word comes out from his mouth discerning truth, rebuking, admonish-
ing, praising, and inviting. He is One who is both human—he
died—and divine. He is One who is able to hold the churches in his
hand.

The fundamental symbol for Jesus in Revelation is that of the lamb
who has been slain. It is used twenty-eight times for Christ in Revelation. "Lamb" in Revelation refers to Christ's saving death on the cross.
The Lamb was slain for the salvation of mankind. By his blood he has
redeemed persons from every tribe, people, and nation to God and
made them a kingdom and priests to God. They shall reign on the earth
(chapter 5). Everywhere that the Lamb is mentioned regardless of what
else is stated about him, John intends and assumes that the hearer will

understand that it is the Lamb who has been slain that is meant.

The Lamb is worthy of worship as is God himself (4-5). The Twenty-four Elders fall down before the Lamb and are joined in singing praises to him by the Four Living Creatures, innumerable companies of angels, and every creature in all creation. The Lamb occupies the same throne with God. Together with God, he is the temple of the New Jerusalem and the light of the city. He is also Judge; he punishes wrong doers. His wrath is the same as God's. The water of life in the new Eden flows from their joint throne.

Not only is the Lamb the sacrificial Lamb that deals with sin and brings salvation, he is also the shepherd and guide of the Christian flock. He is the leader of the 144,000 on Mount Zion (14) and has twelve apostles (21:14). He is also bridegroom and husband of the church (19:7, 9; 21:9).

The Lamb is the initiator of the divine drama of the End (6:1, etc.). He opens the seven seals one by one. As Lord of lords and King of kings he is the conqueror of the Monster, the False Prophet, and the kings of the earth.

John and his fellow Christians in the churches in Asia are able to face victoriously the crisis that is coming upon them by their faith in the Lamb who redeemed them by his death on the cross, who was resurrected, who now is present in their midst to comfort, praise, admonish, protect, to save from their sins, and to conquer the forces of Satan and his earthly deputies. The Lamb will guide his faithful followers to springs of living water (7:17).

John's teaching on the Holy Spirit is more indirect than direct and more a matter of experience than of reflection. His primary experience of the Spirit was in being caught up in a spirit of ecstasy such as experienced by Paul (2 Corinthians 12:2). In the Spirit on the isle of Patmos, he sees the vision of a Son of Man. In the Spirit he is caught up to heaven (4:2), taken away to the wilderness (17:3), and carried to a high mountain where he sees the Holy City (21:10). It is the Spirit that inspires John and other prophets and enables them to see what God wishes them to reveal to the people.

John not only shared with his fellow Christians in the churches of Asia a basic commitment to God and to Jesus Christ, but he also shared tribulation with them. By tribulation he was thinking about the troubles which they could expect. This included the great tribulation of the end-time.

John's basic understanding of history and of life involves a tremendous battle between good and evil. God, and the Lamb are locked in a spiritual struggle with the Devil. Its outcome will determine the destiny of every person. This battle between superhuman forces is mirrored in the visible struggle of the church with the Roman empire.

For John and the churches the present was a mixed bag. He had been a political exile on Patmos because of his faith. The churches experienced a variety of troubles: apathy; false teachers; the lure of riches; the seductive temptation to compromise in the face of social, economic, and political pressure; and apostasy. They also suffered at the hands of their Jewish neighbors and the Roman government. Already Antipas had been martyred.

John expected the situation to get worse. He foresaw a political leader with authority "over every tribe and people and tongue and nation" who would war against the church and conquer it (13:7). Allied with that leader would be the "False Prophet" disguised as a lamb who would perform miracles, promote idolatry, and make all persons worship the leader. It seems clear that John expected the church to suffer strong opposition at the hands of the Roman government even to the point of martyrdom. The situation would become so bad that even commercial and social interchange would be controlled by the government in the interest of loyalty to the emperor. A large number would be martyred and thereby become conquerors and stand before God's throne and sing the victory hymn of Moses and the Lamb. Behind the tribulations experienced and expected on earth, John sees supernatural forces. When the Devil is cast out of heaven to earth, he proceeds to persecute the Glorious Mother and her offspring, the church. So the troubles and persecution John and the churches are suffering is understood as the work of the Devil carried out through his henchmen, the emperor and the priesthood of the cult of Roma.

The number of the martyrs grows. They cry out for vengeance (6:10). Their prayers are answered in the coming of the great day of the wrath of God and of the Lamb (6:17). The tribulation suffered by the Christians is balanced by the plagues of the wrath of God that are to fall on their persecutors. The wrath of God falls on the earth-dwellers, those who bear the brand of the Monster on their hand or forehead (16:2, etc.). The true people of God are protected from his wrath by being sealed on their foreheads (7:3).

The intensity of the plagues increases as the end grows nearer. The final chapters of Revelation blow up in large format the fulfillment of the wrath of God. Babylon, i.e., Rome, portrayed as the Great Prostitute (17:1 — 19:10), is drunk with the blood of saints and the blood of martyrs (17:6). She is to receive a double draught of the wrath of God (18:6). The Monster and the False Prophet are thrown alive into the lake of fire that burns with brimstone (19:20). The wrath finally falls on the supernatural power behind the earthly subordinates, i.e., on the Devil himself and his cohorts. He is thrown into the lake of fire and brimstone (20:10). With the last judgment, the wrath of God falls on anyone whose name is not written in the book of life. They are thrown into the lake of fire (20:15).

John understood the wrath of God to be: 1. punishment on the wicked earth-dwellers for what they had done (20:13; 19:2; 18:7), 2. recompence for the martyrs (6:10; 19:2), 3. motivation intended to bring the wicked to repentance. This is implied by 9:20; 16:9-11; and by the limited destruction in the plagues of the seven trumpets (8-9). However the wicked do not repent.

Repentance for wayward church members is pictured as a much more likely possibility. The basic message of the letters to the churches is "remember," "repent," and "do." It is much more difficult to conceive of your enemies repenting than your fellow Christians. The general atmosphere of determinism which permeates much of Revelation is tempered not only here, but also in chapter 22 where "the leaves of the tree (of life) were for the healing of the nations" (v. 2). Those who are thirsty are invited by Christ to "take the water of life without price" (v. 17).

Thus the immediate goal of Revelation is to bring the members and the members of the congregations in Asia Minor to repentance and faith. "Repent. . . . Be faithful unto death, and I will give you the crown of life!"

The ultimate goal of the book of Revelation is the establishment of the kingdom of God on earth (5:10; 11:15; 19:1-10). In fact the establishment of God's kingdom on earth is the goal of the entire Bible. Only in Revelation, it is finally accomplished.

The basic question for Revelation and for that matter for the Bible as a whole is who is Lord, God or Satan, Caesar or Christ? John paints his answer in a three-step progression. With the defeat of the Devil by Michael and his angels, the kingdom of God is triumphant in heaven. "Now the salvation and the power and the kingdom of our God and the authority of his Christ have come . . . " (12:10).

The second step takes place on earth. Christ, the Word of God, conquers Satan's followers, the Monster, the False Prophets, and the kings of the earth. The Devil himself is imprisoned. Christ and the victorious martyrs reign on earth (19:11 — 20:6).

In the final step, the supernatural powers are defeated. The Devil, Death, and Hades are thrown into the lake of fire and brimstone. The way is cleared for the lordship of God and of Christ to be manifested and the kingdom to appear.

John sees a New Heaven and a New Earth and the New Jerusalem coming down from God. It is his kingdom. He is still on the throne (21:5) and the Lamb is enthroned with him (22:3). The victorious Christians serve God, see his face, and reign for ever and ever (22:4-5).

The sequence of events sketched above does not do justice to John's thought, to the biblical view of God's sovereignty, nor to the theological need for undergirding his fellow Christians in the seven churches of Asia. John never really had any question about God's sovereignty. The only question was when would God take up the slack in the rope and finish off the Devil.

John is so convinced of the eternal sovereignty of God that he can speak of the death of Jesus as "the Lamb slain from the foundation of the world" (13:8). The worship scenes in God's court in heaven make it clear that John believed that even in the present, God reigns as king in heaven (chapters 4 and 5). Not even the highly symbolic battle in heaven between Michael and his angels and Satan and his followers suggests for John that the sovereignty of God is in any real way threatened. In no way was the Great Red Dragon able to snatch the Messiah. God's throne was more than adequate protection (12:1-6).

Again and again throughout Revelation there are clear indications that the kingdom has in some real sense already come. Salvation has already been won. Faithful Christians are already saved; they are already in his kingdom, and priests of God (1:6). Christ is even now present in the midst of the churches of Asia (1:12-13). The presence of Christ and of the kingdom is not yet seen by all. It is seen by "the eyes of faith." What remains is for the eternal, the invisible, which is the real, to become visible to all. The kingdom is coming, and yet it is here. Christ is present and yet he is coming. The first fruits are manifest now; the full harvest is awaited.

In the same way throughout the book, there are previews of the end presented as if they have already occurred. In the midst of the plagues of the seven trumpets, the martyrs are pictured in heaven before the throne serving God (7:9-17). The same language used in describing their situation is used in describing the blessed state of the redeemed in the New Heaven and the New Earth (21:4). Already in chapter 11:15f.

loud voices in heaven proclaim, "The kingdom of the world has become the kingdom of our Lord and of his Christ! . . . " (Cf. 12:10; 19:1-6).

This was John's faith. He had eyes to see the invisible. He had ears to hear the commands of Christ and the will to obey. He wrote that his fellow brothers and sisters in the seven churches might have the eyes of faith to see the Almighty enthroned in heaven as sovereign of the universe, eyes to see the Glorified Christ in the midst of the churches. He wrote that they might have ears to hear the commands of Christ and his promise of a new name, hidden manna, and a place in the temple of God in the new Jerusalem. John wrote that his fellow Christians might have the courage to be faithful unto death and to receive the crown of life. They shared with him the *tribulation*. He wanted them to share also the *unflinching loyalty* so that they might share with him the *kingdom* (1:9). Even now Christ stands at the heart's door and knocks awaiting an invitation to come in and share in table fellowship (3:21). Once again he issues the invitation, "Come, you who are thirsty. Come take the water of life freely without price" (22:17).

John's concern reaches far beyond the appeal to the individual member. It is an urgent summons to the corporate body of the churches to reconstitute themselves around their former love, to "turn around," i.e., repent. It reaches to the struggle of the church with the political and religious powers confronting them in the Roman empire. Even more, it reaches to the supernatural struggle with the demonic forces of Satan that John understands as lying behind the struggle of the churches with the powers of evil within and without.

John issues a clarion call, "Repent! Turn around! Return to your former love for Christ! Confront the Roman empire! Stand fast! Be faithful unto death! The powers you struggle with are greater than their earthly pawn, the Roman empire. You are fighting against Satan and his demonic powers. But be of good cheer. Christ is risen! Christ rules! God has taken into his hands the reins of the universe. Already Satan has been conquered in Heaven. Christ will soon defeat him on earth. The kingdom of God is coming. So be faithful unto death and I will give you the crown of life. Stand fast!"

Throughout the history of the Christian church whenever she has faced social and political upheaval, she has found comfort, renewed courage, and faith through returning to these words of John in the book of Revelation. Our age is no exception. Confronted by political and religious persecution, by social upheaval, by the ravages of war, by economic forces beyond her control, by the increasing threat of atomic

weapons, hydrogen and neutron bombs, the church is turning again to
the message of John. Above and beyond the "super powers," the "military-industrial complex," the international cartels, the disintegration of
the ethical foundations of society, the church proclaims, "God is on the
throne!" The Lamb has redeemed persons from every nation an innumerable company of the faithful. "The Glorified Resurrected Christ"
is walking amid the churches. He is Victor. He has decisively defeated
the powers of evil. His kingdom is coming.

It is in repentance. It is in faithful living in response to this expectant hope that the church finds its life today.

Date Due

BRODART, INC.   Cat. No. 23 233   Printed in U.S.A.